MORE RARE AND UNUSUAL KNOWLEDGE

YOU DIDN'T KNOW

DANIEL BULMEZ

Copyright © 2025 DANIEL BULMEZ

All rights reserved.

ISBN: 9798301822360

DEDICATION

For the curious at heart:

To those who find wonder in the ordinary,
who see questions in the everyday,
and who seek the stories behind the seams of life.

This book is for you, the explorers of the mundane,
the seekers of the hidden histories,
and the lovers of life's little mysteries.

May your curiosity always be your guide,
and may every page turn reveal a new horizon of knowledge.

With gratitude,

.

CONTENTS

i	Introduction	vi
1	**Chapter 1: Animal Kingdom**	**1**
	Peculiar behaviors in animals.	2
	Unusual animal friendships.	6
	Extinct animals with odd features.	9
2	**Chapter 2: Plant Life**	**15**
	Plants that can eat animals.	16
	Trees with medicinal properties.	19
	Flowers with unique pollination methods.	22
3	**Chapter 3: Earth's Wonders**	**25**
	Geological phenomena (e.g., underwater volcanoes, quicksand).	31
	Natural formations (e.g., longest caves, deepest lakes).	32
	Weather anomalies (e.g., fire whirls, ball lightning).	35
4	**Chapter 4: Historical Curiosities**	**41**
	Misconceptions about famous historical events.	42
	Surprising facts about famous figures.	50
	Unexpected inventions (e.g., the microwave was discovered by accident).	61
5	**Chapter 5: Science and Technology**	**71**
	Breakthroughs that changed daily life (e.g., the internet).	72
	Lesser-known scientists and their contributions.	85
	Futuristic technologies that exist today.	91

6	**Chapter 6: Art and Culture**	101
	Unique traditions from around the world.	102
	Bizarre or forgotten art movements.	108
	Music facts that will surprise you.	112
7	**Chapter 7: Space Facts**	119
	Oddities about planets in our solar system.	120
	Strange astronomical events.	125
	Space travel myths and realities.	131
8	**Chapter 8: Cosmic Conundrums**	139
	Theories about the universe's end.	140
	The concept of time in space.	143
	Alien life speculation.	146
9	**Chapter 9: Food and Drink**	149
	Origins of common foods.	150
	Strange food laws around the world.	159
	Historical diets that might shock you.	162
10	**Chapter 10: Language and Words**	165
	Words with surprising origins.	166
	Phrases that have changed meanings over time.	173
	The world's most difficult languages to learn.	177

Introduction: Unveiling the Secrets of the Ordinary

Welcome to **"A World of Wonders: Fun and Fascinating Facts"**, where the extraordinary meets the everyday, and the mundane reveals its magic. This book is your passport to a journey through the realms of the peculiar, the profound, and the downright surprising elements of our planet and beyond.

In an age where information is at our fingertips, yet often overlooked due to the sheer volume available, this collection aims to capture your curiosity, providing you with a treasure trove of tidbits that are both enlightening and entertaining. From the depths of our oceans to the far reaches of space, from the ancient past to the cutting edge of modern science, these pages contain stories, facts, and phenomena that will challenge your understanding and expand your worldview.

Why are facts interesting? Because they represent the building blocks of knowledge. They offer us a glimpse into the complexity of life, the intricacies of nature, and the boundless creativity of human endeavor. Through understanding these facts, we not only enhance our knowledge but also our ability to engage in meaningful conversations, impress others at social gatherings, or simply marvel at the universe's vast and unpredictable tapestry.

This book is structured to guide you through various facets of our existence:

- **The Natural World** invites you into the kingdom of animals, plants, and Earth's geological wonders, exploring the bizarre behaviors, medicinal properties, and natural anomalies that shape our planet.
- **Human Achievements** delves into the historical curiosities, technological breakthroughs, and cultural marvels that define our species, offering a look at how we've shaped the world and how it has shaped us in return.
- **The Universe and Beyond** takes you on a cosmic journey, exploring the mysteries of our solar system, the enigmas of the universe's end, and the speculative realms of alien life.
- **Everyday Wonders** examines the origins of common foods, the evolution of language, and miscellaneous facts that might not fit neatly into categories but are too fascinating to ignore.

Each chapter is designed not just to inform but to inspire wonder, curiosity, and perhaps a bit of laughter. Remember, the world is full of wonders waiting to be discovered, and every fact you learn is a step closer to appreciating the intricate beauty of life and the universe. Whether you're here for trivia night ammunition, to satisfy your innate curiosity, or just for the joy of learning, "A World of Wonders" is your guide to seeing the world through a lens of astonishment.

So, prepare to be amazed, amused, and perhaps a little astounded as we embark together on this delightful detour through the known, the unknown, and the unexpectedly wonderful. Enjoy the journey!

RARE AND UNUSUAL KNOWLEDGE

CHAPTER 1

ANIMAL KINGDOM

RARE AND UNUSUAL KNOWLEDGE

Peculiar Behaviors in Animals

The animal kingdom is full of surprises, where creatures exhibit behaviors that can range from the utterly bizarre to the deeply touching. Here are some of the most peculiar behaviors observed in the wild:

Playing Dead: Several species, like the opossum and the hognose snake, have mastered the art of thanatosis, or playing dead. When threatened, the opossum will lie still, its body going limp, tongue hanging out, and even emitting a foul smell to deter predators. It's nature's dramatic performance to avoid becoming a meal.

Anting by Birds: Birds like starlings and crows engage in a behavior called anting, where they either rub ants into their feathers or lie on ant nests. The formic acid from the ants is believed to help control parasites, but it could also simply be for the sensation or even for defensive purposes.

The Dancing Bees: Honeybees perform a "waggle dance" to communicate with their hive mates about the location of nectar sources. The dance's pattern, including the angle of the waggle relative to the sun, conveys distance and direction. It's one of the most sophisticated forms of communication in the animal world.

Crows Holding Funerals: American crows have been observed gathering around their dead, leading to what looks like a funeral. This gathering might serve to learn about the cause of death, to reinforce social bonds, or to investigate potential dangers in the area.

Giraffe Birth: Rather than giving birth on the ground, which could endanger both mother and baby from predators, giraffes give birth standing up. The calf drops approximately 5 feet to the ground, which might seem harsh but is thought to stimulate the newborn to breathe and stand quickly.

Bowerbird's Artistry: Male bowerbirds create elaborate structures, or bowers, decorated with colorful objects to attract mates. It's not just about the structure; the arrangement and color coordination play a crucial role, showcasing an aesthetic sense unique in the animal kingdom.

Octopus Using Coconut Shells: The veined octopus in Indonesia has been observed using coconut shells as mobile homes. They carry these shells across the ocean floor to use as shelter, demonstrating a level of tool use and planning previously thought to be beyond their capabilities.

Cross-Species Adoption: In the wild, there are instances of animals caring for offspring not of their own species. For example, a lioness in Kenya adopted a baby oryx, an antelope species, protecting it from predators and integrating it into her pride for a time.

Elephant Burial Grounds: While not entirely accurate, elephants do exhibit unique behaviors towards their dead. They will often revisit the bones of their deceased, caressing the bones with their trunks, suggesting a complex understanding of death and memory.

Parrot Parenting: Some parrots, like the African grey, will deliberately lay eggs in nests where other parrots are already incubating. This increases the chances of at least some of their offspring surviving, even if it means relying on others to raise them.

Dolphins Using Tools: In Shark Bay, Australia, dolphins have been seen using marine sponges as tools to forage for food. They put a sponge on their snout to protect it while searching for fish on the sea floor, a behavior passed down through generations.

Otters Holding Hands: Sea otters sleep while floating on their backs. Sometimes, they hold hands or wrap themselves in seaweed to prevent drifting apart while they rest.

Puffer Fish Circles: Male puffer fish create intricate sand patterns on the seafloor to attract mates, demonstrating an artistic flair in underwater courtship.

Sloth's Bathroom Trip: Three-toed sloths descend from the trees just once a week to defecate, a risky journey that might be related to maintaining their personal hygiene or fertilizing the algae in their fur.

Mantis Shrimp's Color Vision: The mantis shrimp has the most complex vision system known, seeing colors beyond what humans can perceive, including ultraviolet and polarized light.

Penguins Proposing with Pebbles: Male Adélie penguins will search for the smoothest, most attractive pebbles to offer to a female as a proposal for mating.

Gorilla's Beatboxing: Western lowland gorillas have been observed making vocalizations that sound remarkably like beatboxing, showcasing their vocal versatility.

Flamingo's Yoga: Flamingos often stand on one leg, a behavior that might help them conserve body heat, reduce fatigue in the other leg, or even confuse predators.

Lemmings' Group Suicide Myth: Contrary to popular belief, lemmings do not commit mass suicide. The myth likely stems from their mass migrations where some might fall or be pushed off cliffs due to overcrowding.

Cuttlefish Hypnosis: Some cuttlefish species can hypnotize prey with changing patterns on their skin, mesmerizing crabs or small fish before capturing them.

Magpie's Mirror Self-Recognition: Magpies, like some primates, can recognize themselves in mirrors, indicating a level of self-awareness rare among animals.

Elephants and Names: Elephants use distinct sounds to address each other individually, similar to how humans use names, showcasing a complex social communication system.

Rocking Horseshoe Crabs: Horseshoe crabs use their tail to flip themselves over if they end up upside down, but some species also bob or rock their bodies to signal health during mating.

Bats Adopting Orphans: Vampire bats have been known to adopt orphaned pups by sharing food through regurgitation, highlighting their social support system.

Crows and Gifts: Crows, known for their intelligence, sometimes leave gifts for humans who have been kind to them, indicating a form of gratitude or memory.

Whale's Bubble Net Fishing: Humpback whales create a ring of bubbles to trap fish, then swim up through the center with their mouths open, a coordinated and learned hunting technique.

Ants Farming Fungus: Leafcutter ants cultivate a specific type of fungus in underground gardens for food, showing a form of agriculture in the insect world.

Dancing Spiders: The peacock spider performs a vibrant dance, displaying its colorful abdomen to attract mates, a spectacle of courtship in the arachnid world.

Octopus Ink as Disguise: Not just for escape, some octopuses use their ink to create decoys or "pseudomorphs" that mimic their shape, providing a diversion.

Fish Using Tools: The archerfish spits jets of water to knock insects out of the air, using water as a tool from a distance.

Sharks' Electroreception: Sharks can detect electrical fields in water, which helps them find prey even when it's buried or hidden, showing an extraordinary sensory ability.

Unusual Animal Friendships

In the wild, where survival often dictates the rules, one might expect only competition and predation. However, nature occasionally surprises us with stories of interspecies friendships that defy these expectations. Here are some heartwarming examples:

Baboon and Bush Baby: In a South African nature reserve, a baboon was observed adopting an orphaned bush baby, grooming it, and carrying it around. Despite their typical roles in the food chain, this baboon showed remarkable care towards the tiny, nocturnal primate.

Tiger and Orangutan: In a zoo setting, a Bengal tiger and an orangutan developed a bond where they would play together. This friendship showcases how boundaries can blur when animals grow up together in a safe environment.

Dog and Dolphin: In Ireland, a stray dog and a dolphin in a harbor formed an unlikely friendship, playing together regularly. The dolphin would surface to interact with the dog, showcasing the playful side of both species.

Hippo and Tortoise: After losing its mother, a baby hippo named Owen befriended a 130-year-old tortoise named Mzee at a Kenyan wildlife sanctuary. They became inseparable, with Owen treating Mzee as a surrogate parent, despite the vast differences in their species.

Cat and Crow: In Russia, a cat named Romasha and a crow named Pacha became friends. The crow would fly down to the cat, and they would share food, illustrating how companionship can form between natural adversaries.

Bear and Wolf: In the wilderness of Finland, a brown bear and a wolf were spotted not only tolerating each other but also playing together. These instances, while rare, show that even in nature, peace can exist between predators.

Goat and Rhino: At an animal sanctuary, a blind goat named Mr. G and a retired circus rhinoceros named Tank formed a bond. Mr. G would follow Tank, using him as a guide, and they would often graze together, providing comfort to each other.

Eagle and Fox: In a rare sighting, a golden eagle and a red fox were seen sharing a meal. Eagles usually prey on foxes, but this moment captured a peaceful coexistence and shared interest in immediate survival over predation.

Parrot and Dog: A green-winged macaw and a golden retriever demonstrated a deep bond where the parrot would groom the dog, and they would sleep together, showing how companionship transcends species boundaries in domestic settings.

Lions and Hyena: In Tanzania, a pride of lions adopted a baby hyena after its mother was killed. Surprisingly, the lions did not harm the hyena but protected it, even from other hyenas.

Deer and Rabbit: A video went viral showing a wild deer and a rabbit sharing a moment where the deer licked the rabbit in what appeared to be an affectionate gesture, proving that gentle interactions can occur even without any apparent need for survival.

Elephant and Sheep: In an Indian forest, an elephant was seen playing with a sheep, gently picking it up with its trunk and placing it back on the ground. This gentle interaction defies the typical predator-prey dynamics.

Cat and Dolphin: At a seaside cafe in Turkey, a cat named Dushka often visited to interact with dolphins in the harbor. The dolphins would approach the pier, and Dushka would play with them, showing interspecies playfulness.

Cow and Pig: On a farm, a cow and a pig were observed lying down together for warmth, their friendship providing mutual comfort and companionship.

Dog and Duck: In an animal rescue in the UK, a dog named Fred and a duck named Jemima became companions. Fred would guard Jemima, and they would often nap together, showcasing a protective bond.

Seal and Penguin: In a South African zoo, a seal took to a baby penguin, gently moving it around with its flippers, playing without the usual predatory instincts.

Horse and Chicken: On a farm in the United States, a horse named Jingles and a chicken named Peep became inseparable. Peep would often ride on Jingles' back, pecking at ticks, which seemed to bother the horse less than usual.

Owl and Cat: An owner's pet owl and cat developed a friendship where the owl would perch on the cat, and they would often cuddle, defying their natural roles as predator and prey.

Polar Bear and Husky: In a zoo, a polar bear cub and a husky puppy grew up together, playing like siblings. The bear would mimic the dog's behavior, showing how early companionship can influence behavior.

Squirrel and Rabbit: A garden in Canada became home to an unusual friendship where a squirrel would visit a rabbit, sharing food and playing together, surprising onlookers with their conviviality.

Goose and Mallard Duck: A lone goose found companionship with a mallard duck, swimming together, preening each other, and even sharing nesting duties, highlighting how loneliness can lead to cross-species bonds.

Pig and Tortoise: On an animal sanctuary, a pig named Wilbur and a tortoise named Shelldon would spend their days together. Wilbur would lie next to Shelldon, providing warmth during cooler days.

Swan and Crane: At a wildlife reserve, a swan and a crane formed an unusual alliance, often seen swimming side by side, feeding together, and showing protective behaviors towards each other.

Raccoon and Cat: A raccoon in an urban backyard setting befriended a cat, sharing food, playing, and even grooming each other. This friendship showed how animals can adapt to urban environments and form bonds across species lines.

Extinct Animals with Odd Features

The annals of paleontology are filled with creatures that seem straight out of science fiction, with features so bizarre that they challenge our understanding of evolution. Here are some extinct animals known for their peculiar attributes:

Thylacine (Tasmanian Tiger):

Stripes: Despite its name, it had stripes reminiscent of a tiger.

Pouch: As a marsupial, it had a pouch, yet it looked more like a canine, showcasing convergent evolution.

Glyptodon:

Armor: This massive armadillo relative had a shell made of bony plates, similar to a turtle, but it was the size of a small car.

Tail Club: It wielded a club-like tail, presumably for defense.

Dodo:

Flightlessness: Evolved on an island with no predators, it lost the ability to fly over time.

Large Beak: Its beak was hooked and large, adapted for eating fruits, seeds, and small creatures.

Hallucigenia:

Spikes: This tiny Cambrian creature had spines along its back, with its body orientation initially misunderstood by scientists.

Legs and Appendages: It had seven pairs of tentacles, which were initially thought to be legs, and a head that was only later identified correctly.

Archaeopteryx:

Feathers: Recognized as one of the earliest birds, it had feathers, but also...

Teeth: Unlike modern birds, it had teeth in its beak.

Claws on Wings: Its wings ended in claws, suggesting a transition from dinosaur to bird.

Quetzalcoatlus:

Size: With a wingspan up to 10 meters, it was one of the largest flying animals ever.

Long Neck: Its neck was elongated, possibly for hunting small prey while flying.

Paraceratherium:

Hornless Rhinoceros: This was the largest land mammal known, related to rhinoceroses but without the horn.

Long Legs: It had disproportionately long legs, making it look somewhat giraffe-like from a distance.

Titanis Walleri (Terror Bird):

Height: Standing up to 10 feet tall, these flightless birds were apex predators.

Large Beak: They had a massive, hatchet-shaped beak designed for crushing prey.

Stethacanthus:

Strange Fin: This prehistoric shark had a dorsal fin that looked like an anvil, possibly used in mating displays or combat.

Denticles: Its skin was covered in small, tooth-like scales, providing an odd texture.

Opabinia:

Five Eyes: It had five eyes, a feature so unusual it makes us question its function.

Proboscis: A unique tube-like proboscis with a claw at the end, used for feeding.

Aegyptopithecus:

Pronounced Canines: This early primate had large canines, but also...

Tail: It had a long tail, a feature less common in modern primates.

Phorusrhacidae (Terror Birds):

Speed: Some species could run at speeds up to 37 mph, using their legs to catch prey.

Claws: Equipped with large, sharp claws on their toes for grasping or tearing at prey.

Attercopus Fimbriunguis:

Spider-like: One of the earliest known relatives of spiders, but it had...

Tail: A long tail, making it look quite different from modern spiders.

Anomalocaris:

Size: One of the top predators of the Cambrian period, with some species reaching up to 2 meters in length.

Pincer-like Appendages: It had spiny, pincer-like appendages for grasping prey, with a unique, almost alien-like appearance.

Thylacosmilus:

Sabre-Teeth: This marsupial had saber-teeth that grew from the side of its mouth, curving outward, unlike any other saber-toothed animal.

Basilosaurus:

Whale with Legs: Though called a "lizard king," it was actually an early whale with vestigial hind limbs, indicating its tetrapod ancestry.

Meganeura:

Giant Dragonfly: With a wingspan up to 75 cm, this ancient insect could have been a formidable predator.

Dunkleosteus:

Shearing Jaws: This armored fish had jaws that could exert a bite force of 8,000 psi, capable of shearing through bone with self-sharpening plates.

Doedicurus:

Tail Weapon: Similar to the Glyptodon but with a spiked, club-like tail for defense.

Nothosaurus:

Paddle-like Limbs: A marine reptile with long, paddle-shaped limbs for swimming, but also had sharp teeth for catching prey.

Drepanosaurus:

Bizarre Forelimb: One forelimb was much larger than the other, ending in a large claw, possibly used for climbing or capturing prey.

Ambulocetus:

Walking Whale: This early whale could walk on land with its four legs and swim in the water, a transitional form between land mammals and whales.

Brontornis:

Giant Beak: Another terror bird, but with an even more massive beak, designed to crush and possibly decapitate smaller animals.

Inostrancevia:

Giant Canines: A gorgonopsid with large saber-like canines, one of the top predators of its time in the Permian period.

Eryops:

Tusks: An amphibian with large tusks, possibly used in combat or mating displays.

Pulmonoscorpius:

Giant Scorpion: This species could grow up to 2.5 feet long, making it one of the largest known scorpions.

Tullimonstrum (Tully Monster):

Proboscis with Teeth: A soft-bodied creature with a long, proboscis-like snout ending in a toothed jaw, its classification remains a mystery.

Macrauchenia:

Trunk-like Nose: An odd-toed ungulate with a trunk-like snout, suggesting a lifestyle similar to that of modern tapirs or elephants.

Platybelodon:

Shovel-like Tusks: An elephant relative with a lower jaw that ended in a pair of broad, flat tusks resembling a shovel, used for feeding.

Pterygotus:

Giant Claws: This ancient sea scorpion had claw-like appendages that could reach over a meter in length, making it a fearsome predator.

These extinct animals, with their unique and sometimes bizarre adaptations, provide fascinating insights into the evolutionary paths that life has taken. They showcase how diverse and inventive evolution can be in shaping life forms to fit various ecological niches, many of which we can only imagine in the ancient world they inhabited.

CHAPTER 2

PLANT LIFE

Plants that Can Eat Animals

The world of carnivorous plants is as fascinating as it is macabre, where flora turns the tables on the typical predator-prey relationship. Here are some of the most intriguing plants that have evolved to supplement their diet with animal proteins:

Venus Flytrap (Dionaea muscipula):

Trigger Mechanism: It has leaves with hinged lobes that snap shut when sensitive hair-like structures are touched by prey, capturing insects and small spiders.

Digestion: Enzymes are then secreted to digest the trapped creature, with the plant reabsorbing the nutrients.

Pitcher Plants (Nepenthes spp., Sarracenia spp.):

Slippery Rim: The inside of their modified leaves forms a pitfall trap with a slippery rim that causes insects to fall into a pool of digestive enzymes and water at the base.

Variety: Some species can even digest small mammals like rats, showing an incredible adaptation in size and capability.

Sundews (Drosera spp.):

Sticky Tentacles: Their leaves are covered with glandular hairs that exude a sticky mucilage, trapping insects that land on them.

Movement: The leaves can slowly curl around the prey, maximizing contact for digestion.

Bladderworts (Utricularia spp.):

Bladder Mechanism: They have tiny, bladder-like structures that can suck in water along with small aquatic organisms, using a vacuum-like action triggered by touch-sensitive hairs.

Speed: This trapping mechanism is one of the fastest movements in the plant kingdom, occurring in milliseconds.

Butterworts (Pinguicula spp.):

Mucilage: Their leaves produce a sticky, enzyme-rich mucilage that both traps insects and begins digestion upon contact.

Adaptability: Some species can switch between a carnivorous diet and photosynthesis based on environmental conditions.

Cobra Lily (Darlingtonia californica):

Lobster Pot Trap: Shaped like a cobra's head, it lures insects into its translucent "false exit" where they get confused and fall into the digestive chamber.

No Digestive Enzymes: Interestingly, it doesn't produce enzymes; instead, it relies on symbiotic relationships with bacteria to break down its prey.

Tropical Pitcher Plant (Nepenthes rajah):

Giant Pitchers: It has some of the largest pitchers in the genus, capable of digesting small mammals, birds, and even tree shrews, which also use the pitchers as latrines, benefiting the plant with nitrogen-rich excrement.

Dewy Pine (Drosophyllum lusitanicum):

Sticky Glands: Similar to sundews, but with leaves that grow in a rosette and are densely covered with sticky glands.

No Movement: Unlike some other carnivorous plants, it doesn't move; it relies solely on its sticky surface for capture.

Byblis (Byblis spp.):

Sticky Hairs: Also known as the Rainbow Plant, it has long, sticky hairs that ensnare insects, though it's not as well-known for its predatory nature as some other carnivorous plants.

Catopsis berteroniana:

Bromeliad: A bromeliad that has adapted to a carnivorous lifestyle, capturing insects and small animals within its rosette of leaves where it digests them with the help of enzymes.

Waterwheel Plant (Aldrovanda vesiculosa):

Aquatic Traps: Similar to the Venus flytrap in mechanism but aquatic, it uses its snap traps to catch tiny water creatures.

Australian Pitcher Plants (Cephalotus follicularis):

Unique Shape: Unlike other pitcher plants, it has small, flask-shaped pitchers that resemble a tiny jug, trapping insects in a similar manner.

These plants have evolved in nutrient-poor environments, where capturing and digesting animal life provides them with essential nutrients like nitrogen and phosphorus, which are scarce in their habitats. Their mechanisms for trapping and digesting prey showcase the fascinating adaptability of plant life, turning the tables on the animal kingdom by preying upon it.

Trees with Medicinal Properties

Trees have been humanity's pharmacies long before modern medicine, providing a plethora of compounds with healing properties. Here are some trees known for their medicinal benefits:

Willow (Salix spp.):

Aspirin Precursor: Contains salicin, which is metabolized into salicylic acid in the body, the active ingredient in aspirin, used for pain relief and reducing fever.

Anti-inflammatory: Also used traditionally for its anti-inflammatory effects.

Neem (Azadirachta indica):

Antibacterial: Neem leaves, bark, and seeds have antibacterial properties, useful in treating skin conditions like acne and infections.

Antifungal: Known for its antifungal properties, it's used in treatments for fungal infections.

Dental Care: Twigs are traditionally used as natural toothbrushes for their antimicrobial properties.

Cinchona Tree (Cinchona spp.):

Quinine: The bark contains quinine, an alkaloid used to treat malaria, one of the earliest drugs to be effective against this disease.

Fever Reduction: Historically used for its fever-reducing properties.

Baobab (Adansonia digitata):

Vitamin C: Its fruit is exceptionally high in Vitamin C, boosting the immune system.

Anti-diarrheal: The leaves and seeds have properties that can help in managing diarrhea.

Ginkgo Biloba:

Cognitive Function: Extracts from the leaves are used to enhance memory and cognitive function, particularly in the elderly.

Circulation: It's also believed to improve blood circulation and treat conditions like dementia.

Yew Tree (Taxus baccata):

Paclitaxel: Its bark contains taxol, a compound used in chemotherapy for cancer treatment, particularly breast and ovarian cancers.

Caution: All parts of the yew, except the aril of the berry, are toxic if ingested.

White Willow (Salix alba):

Pain Relief: Similar to other willows but often specifically cited for its use in pain relief, especially for headaches and joint pain.

Sassafras (Sassafras albidum):

Aromatic Oil: The root bark yields safrole, which was once used in root beer for flavor but is now known to be carcinogenic in large amounts.

Medicinal Uses: Historically used for skin conditions, rheumatism, and as a general tonic.

Eucalyptus (Eucalyptus spp.):

Antimicrobial: Oil from the leaves is widely used for its antiseptic and antimicrobial properties, often in treatments for colds, flu, and respiratory issues.

Decongestant: Its vapors are used to clear nasal congestion.

Pau d'Arco (Tabebuia spp.):

Antibiotic: The inner bark has been used as an herbal remedy for infections, particularly yeast infections, and has shown antibiotic properties.

Anti-inflammatory: Also used for its anti-inflammatory effects.

Tea Tree (Melaleuca alternifolia):

Antiseptic: Tea tree oil is renowned for its antiseptic and antifungal properties, used in wound care and skin treatments.

Acne Treatment: Commonly used in products aimed at treating acne due to its ability to fight bacteria.

Birch (Betula spp.):

Diuretic: Birch leaves and sap are used for their diuretic effects, helping with urinary tract infections.

Joint Pain: Birch tar oil has been used traditionally for joint pain, rheumatic conditions.

Moringa (Moringa oleifera):

Nutrient-Rich: While often considered a shrub, some varieties grow into trees; it's packed with vitamins and antioxidants, used for malnutrition and boosting health.

Anti-inflammatory: Its leaves are used in traditional medicine for their anti-inflammatory properties.

Banyan (Ficus benghalensis):

Antidiabetic: Extracts from the bark and leaves are used in traditional medicine for diabetes management.

Wound Healing: Known for its wound healing properties due to the astringent and antimicrobial effects of its latex.

These trees not only contribute to the ecological balance but also offer a treasure trove of natural remedies. Their use in traditional medicine has led to scientific research, often validating their efficacy and leading to the development of new pharmaceuticals. However, it's crucial to approach their medicinal use with knowledge of proper dosages and potential side effects, as the natural doesn't always mean harmless.

Flowers with Unique Pollination Methods

Pollination is essential for the reproduction of flowering plants, and over time, flowers have developed some ingenious and often bizarre methods to ensure their pollen reaches other plants. Here are some flowers with particularly unique strategies:

The Bee Orchid (Ophrys apifera):

Mimicry: It mimics the appearance and scent of female bees to attract male bees for pollination. The males attempt to mate with the flower, inadvertently picking up and depositing pollen.

The Stinking Corpse Lily (Rafflesia arnoldii):

Carrion Flower: Emits a foul odor similar to rotting flesh to attract flies, which act as pollinators. Its large, red, and petal-less structure further mimics decay.

The Titan Arum (Amorphophallus titanum):

Thermal Regulation: This plant can actually heat up its spadix to spread its scent more effectively, attracting flies and beetles with an odor of rotting meat.

The Duck Orchid (Caleana major):

Duck Shape: Its petals and sepals form a shape resembling a duck in flight, which attracts insects by visually deceiving them.

The Hammer Orchid (Drakaea spp.):

Sexual Deception: Utilizes a method similar to the bee orchid but targets male wasps. The flower's labellum looks and smells like a female wasp, leading to 'pseudocopulation' where the male attempts to mate with the flower.

The Fly Ragwort (Senecio aureus):

Nectar Guides: Has UV reflective patterns on its petals that only insects can see, guiding them directly to the nectar and ensuring pollen transfer.

The Barrel Cactus (Ferocactus spp.):

Bat Pollination: Opens mostly at night to be pollinated by bats, which are attracted to its large, white flowers that are easily seen in the moonlight.

The Slipper Orchid (Paphiopedilum spp.):

Trap Mechanism: The labellum forms a pouch or slipper that insects slide into, where they must exit through a narrow passage covered in pollen, ensuring pollination.

The Passionflower (Passiflora spp.):

Trichomes: Has structures that guide pollinators to the nectaries, and after pollination, the anthers twist to deposit pollen on the visitor.

The Aristolochia (Dutchman's Pipe):

Trap and Release: The flower's structure traps insects inside for a short period. As the flower matures, it releases the insects, now dusted with pollen, to pollinate other plants.

The Porcelain Flower (Hoya carnosa):

Nectar Pockets: Produces copious amounts of nectar in specially designed pockets that can only be accessed by insects with long proboscises, like moths.

The Bulbophyllum (Orchid Genus):

Carrion Mimicry: Many species mimic the smell of carrion, attracting flies for pollination. Some even mimic the texture or color of rotting meat.

The Blue-Flowered Tasmanian Mountain Daisy (Brachyscome decipiens):

Insect Mimicry: The flowers look like flies from a distance, possibly deterring herbivores or attracting pollinators that seek out flies.

The Cyclanthaceae Family (e.g., Carludovica palmata):

Beetle Pollination: Flowers open in a way that beetles can enter for shelter, food, and mating, becoming covered in pollen in the process.

The Purple-Flowered Dahlia (Dahlia spp.):

Attracts Butterflies: Has evolved to specifically attract and accommodate butterflies, providing them with landing platforms and nectar, while their bodies brush against the stamens.

These examples showcase the incredible diversity and creativity of nature's solutions to the pollination challenge. Flowers have evolved not just to be visually appealing to humans but to interact with their environment in sophisticated ways that ensure their survival through effective pollen transfer. Each method reflects an adaptation to specific environmental pressures, pollinator availability, and ecological niches.

CHAPTER 3

EARTH'S WONDERS

Geological Phenomena

Our planet is alive with a myriad of geological wonders, each telling a story of Earth's dynamic processes. Here are some fascinating geological phenomena:

Underwater Volcanoes:

Submarine Eruptions: These can form new islands or contribute to the growth of existing ones. The eruption of an underwater volcano can lead to the creation of new ocean floor or affect marine ecosystems dramatically.

Hydrothermal Vents: Often associated with these volcanoes, vents emit hot, mineral-rich water, supporting unique ecosystems where life thrives in extreme conditions.

Quicksand:

Liquefaction: Quicksand forms when water saturates an area of loose sand or silt, reducing its friction and causing it to behave like a liquid. Contrary to popular belief, you won't sink entirely; the human body is less dense than quicksand.

Formation: Commonly found near riverbanks, beaches, or in areas where underground springs flow into dry sand.

The Great Rift Valley:

Tectonic Activity: This vast geological trough is formed by the divergent movements of the African and Arabian tectonic plates, showcasing where continents are pulling apart.

Diverse Landscapes: Features lakes, volcanoes, and some of the oldest geological formations on Earth, illustrating the dramatic forces of continental drift.

Fjords:

Glacial Carving: Fjords are deep, narrow inlets with steep sides or cliffs, created by glaciers moving down a valley and then receding or melting away.

Submergence: When the land rises or sea levels rise, these valleys can become flooded, forming these dramatic inlets.

Karst Landscapes:

Limestone Dissolution: Formed by the dissolution of soluble rocks such as limestone, dolomite, and gypsum, creating unique features like sinkholes, caves, and underground rivers.

Cenotes: In places like the Yucatan Peninsula, karst activity has led to the formation of cenotes, natural pits or sinkholes resulting from the collapse of limestone bedrock.

Lava Tubes:

Volcanic Features: Formed when the outer surface of a lava flow cools and hardens while the interior remains molten and flows out, leaving a hollow tube.

Cave Systems: These tubes can form extensive underground networks, some of which are explored for their geological and ecological significance.

Dunes and Desert Features:

Star Dunes: Found in places like the Sahara, these are the tallest dunes on Earth, formed where winds blow from multiple directions, creating complex star-shaped formations.

Singing Sands: Certain dunes, when disturbed by wind or footsteps, produce a low-frequency sound, known as "booming dunes" or "singing sands."

The Danakil Depression:

Extremes: One of the hottest, lowest, and most inhospitable places on Earth, yet it boasts vibrant colors due to its geological activity, including sulfur springs, acid ponds, and salt lakes.

Volcanic Activity: Active volcanoes, hot springs, and geysers make it a stark reminder of Earth's active geology.

Salt Domes:

Rising Salt: These are formed when salt layers buried deep underground rise through overlying rocks, sometimes piercing the surface, creating unique landforms and influencing oil and gas deposits.

Landscape Features: They can form hills or even islands in the middle of salt flats.

Mud Volcanoes:

Non-Magmatic Eruptions: These volcanoes erupt mud, water, and gases, not lava. They're often found in areas with petroleum deposits, where hydrocarbons and other gases force their way to the surface.

Miniature Landscapes: While some are large, many are small, creating a landscape dotted with what look like miniature volcanoes.

The Ring of Fire:

Volcanic and Seismic Activity: A major area in the basin of the Pacific Ocean where a large number of earthquakes and volcanic eruptions occur, due to the tectonic plates' movements.

Subduction Zones: Includes the deepest oceanic trenches, where one tectonic plate is forced under another, leading to the formation of volcanic arcs and mountain ranges.

Craters (Meteorite Impact Craters):

Impact Sites: Like the Barringer Crater in Arizona, these are scars left by meteorites striking Earth, revealing insights into both cosmic history and Earth's geological past.

Lava Pillows:

Underwater Lava: When lava flows into the sea or other bodies of water, it cools rapidly, forming pillow-like structures. These are crucial for understanding submarine volcanism.

The Great Artesian Basin:

Vast Aquifer: One of the largest underground water reservoirs in the world, stretching across several Australian states, it's a testament to how water can be stored and move within the Earth.

Hoodoo Formations:

Erosion Wonders: Found in places like Bryce Canyon, these are tall, thin spires of rock, shaped by differential erosion of alternating hard and soft rock layers.

The Eye of the Sahara (Richat Structure):

Geological Bull's Eye: A prominent circular feature in the Sahara desert, believed to be formed by uplift and erosion, not an impact crater as once thought.

Antarctica's Dry Valleys:

Ice-Free Deserts: Despite being in Antarctica, these valleys are some of the driest places on Earth, showcasing how extreme conditions can preserve geological features.

The Giant's Causeway:

Hexagonal Columns: Formed by the cooling and cracking of lava flows, resulting in thousands of interlocking basalt columns, an example of columnar jointing.

The Pillars of Hercules:

Strait of Gibraltar: This refers to the promontories that flank the entrance to the Mediterranean Sea, symbolizing the limits of the known world in ancient times.

Travertine Terraces (like those at Pamukkale, Turkey):

Mineral Deposits: Created by the deposition of calcium carbonate from hot springs, these terraces offer a stunning, almost surreal landscape.

The Devil's Tower:

Igneous Intrusion: An isolated igneous butte in Wyoming, USA, it's thought to be formed by the intrusion of magma into surrounding layers of rock, which have since eroded away.

Fairy Chimneys (Cappadocia, Turkey):

Erosion Art: Formed by volcanic eruptions followed by wind and water erosion, these unique rock formations have been hollowed out for centuries to create homes and churches.

The Namib Desert's Fairy Circles:

Mysterious Patterns: Circular patches of bare soil surrounded by grass, their origin remains a subject of scientific debate, possibly related to termite activity or plant competition for water.

The Wave (Arizona/Utah, USA):

Sandstone Wonder: A sandstone rock formation known for its wave-like appearance, formed by erosion of Navajo Sandstone under unique conditions.

The Yellow Dragon (Huanglong, China):

Calcite Pools: Similar to travertine terraces but with vibrant colors due to algae and other microorganisms, creating a dragon-like appearance.

The Basaltic Prisms of Santa María Regla, Mexico:

Columnar Basalt: A series of hexagonal basalt columns formed from cooled lava flows, creating a dramatic natural display reminiscent of a giant's organ.

The Natural Bridge of Virginia:

Karst Feature: One of the oldest natural landmarks in the U.S., formed by the erosion of the surrounding rock, leaving this massive bridge of limestone.

The Pinnacles Desert in Australia:

Limestone Pillars: Thousands of limestone formations, the result of ancient sea shells compacting over time and then being shaped by wind erosion.

The Chocolate Hills in the Philippines:

Unique Landforms: Over 1,200 uniformly shaped mounds that turn brown in the dry season, giving them their name, though their formation remains somewhat mysterious.

These additional geological phenomena not only captivate with their beauty but also provide scientists with natural laboratories for studying Earth's processes. From the fiery beginnings of lava flows to the slow, patient work of wind and water erosion, these features remind us of the dynamic and ever-changing nature of our planet's geology.

Natural Formations

Earth's surface and subsurface are adorned with natural formations that astonish and inspire wonder. These features, sculpted by the forces of nature over millions of years, include some of the planet's most remarkable caves, lakes, and other geological spectacles:

The Longest Cave System: Mammoth Cave, USA:

Extensive Network: With over 405 miles (652 kilometers) of surveyed passageways, Mammoth Cave is the world's longest known cave system, showcasing stalactites, stalagmites, and underground rivers.

The Deepest Cave: Veryovkina Cave, Abkhazia:

Vertical Descent: Descending more than 2,212 meters (7,256 feet), Veryovkina holds the title for the world's deepest cave, challenging cavers with its sheer drops and water-filled sections.

The Deepest Lake: Lake Baikal, Russia:

Depth: Plunging to depths of approximately 1,642 meters (5,387 feet), Lake Baikal contains about 20% of the world's unfrozen surface fresh water, making it the deepest and one of the oldest lakes in the world.

The Giant's Causeway, Northern Ireland:

Basalt Columns: Comprising around 40,000 interlocking basalt columns, this UNESCO World Heritage site was formed by an ancient volcanic eruption and subsequent cooling of lava.

The Great Barrier Reef, Australia:

Coral Wonders: The largest coral reef system, stretching over 2,300 kilometers, it's not just a natural formation but a living organism, teeming with biodiversity.

The Grand Canyon, USA:

River Carving: Carved over millions of years by the Colorado River, this canyon reveals layers of geological history with its depth reaching over a mile in some places.

The Stalactite and Stalagmite Formations of Postojna Cave, Slovenia:

Underground Marvels: One of the largest cave systems in the world where the formations have grown into shapes like curtains, pillars, and the famous "Brilliant" stalagmite.

The Marble Caves of Patagonia, Chile:

Sculpted by Water: Located in General Carrera Lake, these caves are formed from marble and offer mesmerizing blue hues and intricate patterns shaped by millennia of wave action.

The Waitomo Glowworm Caves, New Zealand:

Glowworm Light: Here, the cave roof is illuminated by the bioluminescent glow of countless glowworms, creating an otherworldly starry night effect underground.

The Natural Bridge, Virginia, USA:

Karst Bridge: A massive natural arch of limestone that spans over Cedar Creek, formed through the dissolution and erosion of rock, it stands as a testament to karst processes.

The Eye of Africa (Richat Structure), Mauritania:

Circular Formation: A geological structure in the Sahara desert that from space looks like a bull's eye, believed to be formed by uplift and erosion rather than an impact.

The Fly Geyser, Nevada, USA:

Man-made and Natural: Although initially caused by drilling gone awry, this geyser now erupts continuously, creating colorful mineral deposits and a spectacle of natural beauty.

The Chocolate Hills, Bohol, Philippines:

Unique Topography: Over 1,200 symmetrical mounds that turn brown during the dry season, resembling chocolate kisses, their formation is still debated among geologists.

The Three Sisters, Blue Mountains, Australia:

Sandstone Giants: Three distinct rock formations standing tall amidst the Jamison Valley, formed from a layer of sandstone that has eroded at different rates.

The Danxia Landform, China:

Red Bedrock: Exhibiting layers of red sandstone and conglomerate formed in the Cretaceous period, these formations are known for their vibrant colors and peculiar shapes due to erosion.

The Devil's Kettle, Minnesota, USA:

Mysterious Waterfall: One half of the Brule River flows into a pothole and seemingly disappears, creating a mystery as to where the water goes after falling.

The Tsingy de Bemaraha, Madagascar:

Karst Forest: A forest of limestone needles, pillars, and canyons, this 'stone forest' is one of the most dramatic examples of karst topography in the world.

Each of these natural formations tells a story of Earth's geological history, shaped by forces like erosion, volcanic activity, sedimentation, and tectonic movements. They offer not only stunning visual spectacles but also valuable insights into the processes that continue to shape our planet.

Weather Anomalies

The atmosphere around us is full of wonders and sometimes produces phenomena that are as beautiful as they are mysterious. Here are some of the most intriguing weather anomalies:

Fire Whirls (Fire Tornadoes):

Phenomenon: These occur when intense heat and turbulent wind conditions combine, causing flames to spin rapidly around a central axis, forming what looks like a tornado of fire.

Locations: Often seen in wildfires or large controlled burns, they can also form around industrial fires or in volcanic eruptions.

Ball Lightning:

Mysterious Orbs: Characterized by glowing, floating spheres that appear during thunderstorms, ball lightning can vary in size, color, and duration, sometimes entering homes or airplanes.

Scientific Intrigue: While its exact nature remains elusive, theories suggest it might involve electrical energy interacting with the atmosphere in unique ways.

Hailstones:

Ice Bullets: While hailstorms are not rare, giant hailstones that weigh over a pound or have diameters larger than softballs are anomalies that can cause significant damage.

Formation: They form in thunderstorms with strong updrafts that keep ice particles aloft, allowing them to grow by accumulating layers of supercooled water that freeze upon contact.

Heat Bursts:

Sudden Heat: A rare event where after a thunderstorm, a sudden increase in temperature occurs, sometimes by 10-20 degrees Celsius in minutes, accompanied by strong, dry winds.

Cause: Thought to be related to the rapid descent of cooler mid-level air hitting the ground and warming adiabatically.

Ice Storms:

Glazing Effect: When rain falls through a shallow layer of freezing air, it can turn into ice upon contact with surfaces below, creating a coating of ice that can weigh down trees and power lines, leading to widespread disruption.

Derecho:

Straight-line Winds: A widespread, long-lived wind storm associated with a fast-moving band of severe thunderstorms. Derechos can produce damage equivalent to that of tornadoes over a much larger area.

Saint Elmo's Fire:

Electrical Phenomenon: Named after St. Erasmus (Elmo), this is a weather phenomenon where a luminous plasma glows around pointed objects (like masts of ships or aircraft wings) due to a high electric field gradient, often seen during thunderstorms.

Fata Morgana:

Superior Mirage: These complex mirages can make objects on the horizon (like ships or icebergs) appear to float above the water, caused by temperature inversions creating optical distortions.

Dry Lightning Storms:

No Rain, Just Lightning: Storms where lightning strikes occur, but little to no rain reaches the ground because the rain evaporates before hitting the surface, leading to wildfires in dry conditions.

Volcanic Lightning:

Eruption Sparks: During volcanic eruptions, the friction from ash particles can generate static electricity, leading to spectacular lightning displays within the ash cloud.

The Brocken Spectre:

Giant Shadow: An optical phenomenon where an observer's shadow is cast onto clouds or mist with the head surrounded by a halo-like ring of light, often seen from high places like mountaintops.

Mirages:

Inferior and Superior: Inferior mirages, like those seen on hot roads, make distant objects appear elongated or lifted. Superior mirages can make objects appear higher or even inverted.

Diamond Dust:

Ice Crystals: A ground-level cloud composed of tiny ice crystals that reflect sunlight, creating sparkling effects, especially common in polar regions.

Aurorae (Aurora Borealis and Aurora Australis):

Nature's Light Show: Charged particles from the sun collide with Earth's upper atmosphere, guided by the magnetic field, creating shimmering displays of light in the polar skies.

Moonbows (Lunar Rainbows):

Night Rainbows: Similar to rainbows but formed by moonlight instead of sunlight, they are faint and usually seen in the spray of waterfalls or after rain at night with a full moon.

Catatumbo Lightning:

Almost Continuous: Occurring over the mouth of the Catatumbo River in Venezuela, this phenomenon features lightning strikes almost continuously due to the collision of warm Caribbean winds with cooler mountain air.

Fog Devil:

Miniature Tornado: A small, whirlwind-like vortex that forms in fog, looking like a mini tornado but usually harmless and short-lived.

Dust Devils:

Desert Whirlwinds: Formed in hot, dry conditions, these are small, rotating columns of air made visible by dust, sand, or debris.

Glory (Heiligenschein):

Halo Effect: A circular, rainbow-like effect seen around the shadow of an observer's head, caused by light backscatter from water droplets or ice crystals.

White Rain:

Foggy Descent: Occurs when fog condenses and falls as very light rain, often indistinguishable from mist or drizzle.

Thunder Snow:

Snow with Thunder: Rare, but when cold air aloft meets warm air near the ground, thunderstorms can produce snow instead of rain, accompanied by lightning and thunder.

Frost Foliage:

Ice Crystals: When supercooled water droplets in fog freeze onto surfaces, forming delicate, leaf-like structures of frost.

Fog Arches:

Rare Phenomenon: Similar to moonbows but formed by fog, these are very rare and require specific conditions like a low sun angle and dense fog.

Green Flash:

Optical Trick: A brief green or blue flash seen just as the sun rises or sets, caused by the refraction of light in the atmosphere.

Light Pillars:

Vertical Beams: Columns of light that appear to extend vertically above or below a light source, caused by reflection of light off ice crystals in the atmosphere.

Steam Fog (Sea Smoke):

Cold-Water Vapor: When cold air moves over much warmer water, the water vapor creates a fog that looks like steam or smoke rising from the surface.

Sun Dog (Parhelion):

Mock Suns: Bright spots on either side of the sun, caused by the refraction of sunlight through ice crystals in the atmosphere, often seen with a halo around the sun.

Ice Fogs:

Arctic Phenomenon: In extremely cold conditions, minute ice crystals form in the air, creating a dense fog that can reduce visibility significantly.

Virga:

Rain that Doesn't Reach: Rain or snow that falls from clouds but evaporates before reaching the ground, creating streaks below the cloud.

Haloes:

Atmospheric Rings: Large rings or arcs of light around the sun or moon, formed by the refraction or reflection of light through ice crystals.

Fire Rainbow (Circumhorizontal Arc):

Colorful Display: A rare halo that forms when the sun is high in the sky (more than 58° above the horizon) and its light passes through high-altitude cirrus clouds with plate-shaped ice crystals.

Cold Air Funnel:

Non-Tornadic: A funnel cloud that forms in relatively weak, cold-core systems, not usually associated with severe weather or tornadoes.

Ice Storms:

Freezing Rain: When raindrops fall through a shallow layer of freezing air near the ground, they become supercooled and freeze upon contact, creating a coating of ice.

Mammatus Clouds:

Pouch-like Structures: These clouds form hanging lobes underneath cumulonimbus, often seen after a thunderstorm, their formation involves sinking air.

Aurora in Unusual Colors:

Beyond Green: While green is common, auroras can appear in shades of red, purple, pink, blue, and even yellow, depending on the atmospheric gases involved and the altitude of the interaction.

These weather anomalies showcase the Earth's atmospheric complexity, where conditions can align in such unique ways to produce phenomena that are not only visually stunning but also scientifically fascinating. Each anomaly provides insights into the physical processes of our planet's weather system, reminding us of the ever-changing and sometimes unpredictable nature of the atmosphere.

CHAPTER 4

HISTORICAL CURIOSITIES

Misconceptions about Famous Historical Events

History often gets distilled into simplified narratives, but many of these stories are riddled with inaccuracies or misunderstandings that have been perpetuated over time. Here are some common misconceptions about famous historical events:

The Signing of the Magna Carta:

Misconception: It was a document that granted rights to all Englishmen.

Reality: The Magna Carta was primarily intended to protect the privileges of feudal barons against the king's overreaches, not to establish rights for the common people.

Columbus Discovering America:

Misconception: Christopher Columbus discovered America in 1492.

Reality: Columbus never set foot on mainland North America; he landed in the Bahamas. Additionally, Viking explorers, like Leif Erikson, reached North America centuries earlier.

The Boston Tea Party:

Misconception: It was about protesting high tea prices.

Reality: The event was more about the tax policy and the principle of "no taxation without representation" than the price of tea itself.

The Fall of the Berlin Wall:

Misconception: It fell overnight on November 9, 1989.

Reality: The process began months earlier with the opening of borders and was followed by weeks of chipping away at the wall by both citizens and officials.

Marie Curie's Death:

Misconception: She died from exposure to radiation.

Reality: While her work with radioactive materials likely contributed to her poor health, she officially died of aplastic anemia, a condition exacerbated by her radiation exposure but not solely caused by it.

The Wright Brothers' First Flight:

Misconception: They were the first to fly in a heavier-than-air, powered aircraft.

Reality: Several others, including Samuel Langley, had attempted powered flight, and there are claims by others like Gustave Whitehead that predate the Wrights, though not with as much historical documentation.

The Charge of the Light Brigade:

Misconception: It was a heroic charge that succeeded due to bravery.

Reality: It was a disastrous mistake due to miscommunication, where the brigade charged the wrong target, leading to heavy casualties, yet it's remembered for the soldiers' courage.

The Great Fire of London:

Misconception: It destroyed all of London.

Reality: While devastating, the fire of 1666 destroyed only a part of London, roughly 13,200 houses and 87 churches, but left areas like the City of Westminster untouched.

The Defenestration of Prague:

Misconception: It led directly to the Thirty Years' War.

Reality: While it was a significant event that escalated tensions, the war's causes were much more complex, involving religious, political, and dynastic issues across Europe.

The Signing of the Declaration of Independence:

Misconception: All 56 signers did so on July 4, 1776.

Reality: The declaration was approved by Congress on July 4, but most signers added their names later, some as late as August 2, 1776.

The Sinking of the Titanic:

Misconception: The ship was described as "unsinkable" by its builders.

Reality: While some promotional materials boasted about its safety features, the White Star Line never officially claimed the Titanic was unsinkable.

The Death of Julius Caesar:

Misconception: He was killed because he declared himself king.

Reality: Caesar was assassinated by a group of senators because they feared he was becoming too powerful, not necessarily for declaring himself king, though he was offered the crown.

The Renaissance:

Misconception: It was a sudden, uniform movement across Europe.

Reality: The Renaissance was a gradual process that varied significantly by region, with different focuses and timelines in places like Italy, England, and the Netherlands.

The Burning of the Library of Alexandria:

Misconception: It was destroyed in a single event by Julius Caesar or later by Christians or Muslims.

Reality: The library suffered multiple destructions over centuries, with various culprits including Caesar's fire, Christian riots, and finally, the Muslim conquest, though the extent of each event's damage is debated.

The Discovery of Penicillin:

Misconception: Alexander Fleming discovered penicillin purely by accident when he left a petri dish open.

Reality: While the initial discovery was serendipitous, Fleming had been actively studying bacteria and their interactions with substances, including mold, for years.

The American Civil War Was Only About Slavery:

Misconception: The sole cause of the Civil War was slavery.

Reality: While slavery was a central issue, the war also involved economic differences between the North and South, states' rights, and political power struggles.

Vikings Wore Horned Helmets:

Misconception: Vikings are often depicted with horned helmets.

Reality: There's no archaeological evidence for this. Such helmets were an artistic invention from the 19th century.

The Great Wall of China Is Visible from Space:

Misconception: You can see the Great Wall of China from space with the naked eye.

Reality: This is a myth; it's not visible to the naked eye from space, even from low Earth orbit.

Napoleon Was Short:

Misconception: Napoleon Bonaparte was extremely short.

Reality: He was about 5'2" in French measurements of the time, which is equivalent to about 5'7" in modern measurements, average for his time.

The Salem Witch Trials Were About Women:

Misconception: Only women were accused in the Salem Witch Trials.

Reality: While the majority were women, men were also accused and executed for witchcraft.

Einstein Failed Math:

Misconception: Albert Einstein failed math in school.

Reality: Einstein excelled in math; the story likely stems from confusion with his dislike for rote learning or a misunderstanding of the grading system.

The Bastille Was Full of Political Prisoners:

Misconception: The storming of the Bastille freed many political prisoners.

Reality: There were very few prisoners in the Bastille at the time of its storming, and most were there for common crimes, not political offenses.

The Dark Ages Were a Period of Intellectual Decline:

Misconception: The Early Middle Ages or "Dark Ages" were a time of complete intellectual darkness.

Reality: While there was a decline in some areas, it was also a period of significant development in monastic scholarship, the preservation of ancient texts, and agricultural innovations.

The Spanish Inquisition Was About Burning Heretics:

Misconception: The Spanish Inquisition's primary goal was to burn heretics.

Reality: While it did involve executions, its main aim was also to ensure religious conformity, often through confessions and penance rather than immediate execution.

The Internet Was Invented by Al Gore:

Misconception: Al Gore claimed to have invented the Internet.

Reality: Gore said he had taken the initiative in the early 1990s to make the Internet available to the public and supported its growth, not that he invented it.

The Statue of Liberty Was a Gift from France to America for Independence:

Misconception: It was gifted to celebrate American independence.

Reality: The statue was a gift to represent the friendship between the two nations, and its construction was influenced by the abolition of slavery.

Paul Revere's Midnight Ride:

Misconception: Paul Revere rode alone, shouting "The British are coming!"

Reality: He was one of several riders, and he would have whispered warnings to avoid British capture, not shouted.

The Guillotine Was Invented by Dr. Guillotin:

Misconception: Dr. Joseph-Ignace Guillotin invented the guillotine.

Reality: He proposed the idea for a more humane execution method, but the actual design was developed by others like Dr. Antoine Louis.

The Trojan Horse Was a Greek Invention:

Misconception: The Greeks built the Trojan Horse.

Reality: While in myth it was a Greek stratagem, there's no historical evidence for the event; the story likely serves as a narrative device.

The Founding Fathers Were All Christian:

Misconception: All the American Founding Fathers were devout Christians.

Reality: They had diverse religious beliefs, with some like Thomas Jefferson and Benjamin Franklin being Deists, not orthodox Christians.

Medieval People Believed the Earth Was Flat:

Misconception: Medieval Europeans thought the Earth was flat.

Reality: Many educated people in medieval Europe knew the Earth was spherical, a fact established by ancient Greek scholars and accepted in medieval times.

The Iron Maiden Was a Common Medieval Torture Device:

Misconception: The Iron Maiden was used throughout the Middle Ages.

Reality: There's little evidence for its use in medieval times; it might be a later invention or misunderstanding of other tortures.

The Pyramids Were Built by Slaves:

Misconception: The Egyptian pyramids were constructed by slave labor.

Reality: Evidence suggests they were built by paid laborers, possibly with some use of conscripted workers, not slaves in the sense of chattel slavery.

George Washington Had Wooden Teeth:

Misconception: George Washington had wooden dentures.

Reality: His dentures were made from materials like ivory, lead, human teeth, and possibly animal teeth, but not wood.

The Black Death Was Only Spread by Fleas on Rats:

Misconception: The Black Death was solely spread by fleas on rats.

Reality: While fleas on rats were significant vectors, human-to-human transmission through body lice, direct contact, and respiratory droplets also played a role, particularly in the pneumonic form of the plague.

These corrections highlight how historical narratives can evolve over time, often becoming simplified or dramatized. Acknowledging these nuances helps us understand history with more depth and accuracy.

Surprising Facts About Famous Figures

Albert Einstein:

Patent Clerk: Before becoming renowned for his theory of relativity, Einstein worked as a clerk at the Swiss Patent Office, where he had time to develop many of his ideas.

Cleopatra:

Not Egyptian by Birth: Cleopatra was of Greek descent, part of the Ptolemaic dynasty that ruled Egypt after Alexander the Great's conquest. She was the last pharaoh of Ancient Egypt.

Leonardo da Vinci:

Mirror Writing: He wrote in mirror script, from right to left, which might have been to keep his notes secret or because he was left-handed and found it more comfortable.

Marie Curie:

Shared Nobel: She was the first woman to win a Nobel Prize and the only person to win in two different scientific fields (Physics in 1903 for her work on radioactivity, and Chemistry in 1911 for discovering elements radium and polonium).

Abraham Lincoln:

Patent Holder: Lincoln is the only U.S. president to hold a patent. He invented a device to lift boats over shoals and obstructions in rivers.

Nikola Tesla:

Pigeon Love: Tesla had an unusual attachment to pigeons, particularly a white one that he claimed to love "as a man loves a woman." He would feed them and even had a hotel room set aside for them.

Winston Churchill:

Artistic Endeavors: Churchill was an accomplished painter, producing over 500 paintings. His works were displayed under the pseudonym "Charles Morin" to avoid criticism due to his fame.

Thomas Edison:

X-Ray Experimenter: Edison experimented with X-rays shortly after their discovery, but after burning his hand, he warned against their use, which ironically delayed their medical application in the U.S.

Hedy Lamarr:

Inventor: Beyond her acting career, Hedy Lamarr co-invented a frequency-hopping spread spectrum technology during WWII, which laid foundational work for modern wireless communications like WiFi and Bluetooth.

Mozart:

Scatological Humor: Wolfgang Amadeus Mozart enjoyed scatological humor, often incorporating it into his letters and even some of his compositions.

Isaac Newton:

Alchemist: While known for his work in physics and mathematics, Newton spent a significant amount of his time on alchemy, seeking to transform base metals into gold and find the elixir of life.

Leonardo da Vinci:

Vegetarian: Although not a strict vegetarian by today's standards due to the era's dietary limitations, Leonardo da Vinci had a profound respect for animals, often buying birds in markets only to release them, and wrote extensively on why humans should not eat meat.

Albert Einstein:

No Socks: Einstein reportedly detested wearing socks, claiming they were a waste of time since they always got holes in them, and his big toes would poke through anyway.

Queen Elizabeth I:

Bath Avoidance: Queen Elizabeth I is said to have bathed only once a month, "whether she needed it or not." However, she did use a concoction of rosewater, herbs, and oils for hygiene, which was common for the time.

Vincent van Gogh:

Ear Myth: Contrary to the popular story, van Gogh didn't cut off his entire ear; he cut off a portion of his left earlobe in a fit of madness, possibly to prove his love to a woman.

Abraham Lincoln:

Depression: Lincoln suffered from what we would now call clinical depression, often referred to as "melancholy" in his time. He even wrote about his suicidal thoughts in his early adulthood.

Marie Curie:

Radium's Toll: Her exposure to radiation from her work with radium eventually led to her death from aplastic anemia, a condition where the body stops producing enough new blood cells. Her papers from that time are still radioactive.

Winston Churchill:

Painting as Therapy: Churchill took up painting as a hobby in his 40s to combat depression. He once said, "Painting came to my rescue in a most trying time." He produced over 500 paintings.

Nikola Tesla:

Obsessive Compulsions: Tesla had numerous peculiarities, including an intense fear of germs, a compulsion to do things in threes, and an aversion to touching hair. He also claimed to have visions and a photographic memory.

Cleopatra:

Linguistic Skills: Cleopatra was well-educated and could speak at least nine languages, including Egyptian, which was unusual for a Ptolemaic ruler.

Hedy Lamarr:

Inventor: Known as "the most beautiful woman in the world," Hedy Lamarr co-invented a frequency-hopping system during WWII to prevent enemy forces from jamming radio-controlled torpedoes, a precursor to Wi-Fi, GPS, and Bluetooth technologies.

Thomas Edison:

Sleep Habits: Edison was known for his polyphasic sleep schedule, taking multiple short naps throughout the day rather than sleeping for a long period at night, believing it increased his productivity.

Benjamin Franklin:

Invention of Bifocals: Franklin invented the bifocals after growing frustrated with switching between two pairs of glasses for seeing at different distances. His self-portrait with the glasses might be the earliest known depiction of bifocals.

Friedrich Nietzsche:

Musical Talent: Before his philosophical fame, Nietzsche was a child prodigy in music, composing piano pieces at a young age and even contributing to the music scene at universities.

Sigmund Freud:

Cocaine Advocate: Early in his career, Freud was a proponent of cocaine, seeing it as a cure for many disorders, including depression and morphine addiction. He only later recognized its addictive properties.

Mozart:

Scatological Humor: Mozart had a well-documented interest in scatological humor, incorporating references to bodily functions in his letters and even in some of his music.

George Washington:

Denture Materials: Contrary to the myth of wooden teeth, Washington's dentures were made from materials like ivory, lead-tin, and human teeth, including some purchased from his slaves.

Eleanor Roosevelt:

Secret Love Letter: Eleanor Roosevelt had a close relationship with Lorena Hickok, an AP journalist, evidenced by over 3,000 letters exchanged between them, some hinting at a romantic attachment.

Leon Trotsky:

Ice Axe Assassin: Trotsky was assassinated in Mexico with an ice axe by Ramón Mercader, an agent of Stalin's NKVD, in 1940. The weapon of choice was chosen for its ability to be disguised as an everyday object.

Edgar Allan Poe:

Cryptography Enthusiast: Poe was fascinated by codes and ciphers, even publishing challenges in newspapers for readers to send him cryptograms to solve, which he often did successfully.

Marilyn Monroe:

IQ and Reading: Marilyn Monroe had an IQ of 168 and was an avid reader, with a personal library that included works by James Joyce, Nikolai Gogol, and Fyodor Dostoevsky.

Napoleon Bonaparte:

Fear of Cats: Napoleon suffered from ailurophobia, an intense fear of cats. This fear was so significant that he would lock himself in his room if he saw one.

Albert Einstein:

Violin Skills: Einstein was an accomplished violinist, crediting music with helping him think more clearly and come up with scientific ideas. He once said, "I often think in music. I live my daydreams in music. I see my life in terms of music."

Leonardo da Vinci:

Military Engineering: Despite his more famous artistic contributions, da Vinci spent a significant portion of his career designing weapons of war, including tanks, machine guns, and a self-propelled cart, which was among the first conceptualizations of an automobile.

Frida Kahlo:

Pets: Kahlo had an unusual collection of pets, including spider monkeys, parrots, and even a fawn. These animals often appeared in her paintings, symbolizing various aspects of her life and struggles.

Mahatma Gandhi:

Legal Career: Before his life as a political and spiritual leader, Gandhi studied law in London and practiced in South Africa, where his experiences shaped his philosophy of non-violent resistance.

Amelia Earhart:

Fashion Icon: Earhart was not only a pioneering aviator but also influenced fashion with her preference for practical, comfortable clothing, leading to the creation of a line of clothing by a fashion designer she inspired.

Nikola Tesla:

Sleep Patterns: Tesla claimed he could function on minimal sleep, often taking naps every few days, and he believed this helped him maintain a clear mind for his work.

Elvis Presley:

Twin Brother: Elvis had a stillborn identical twin brother, Jesse Garon Presley. This loss had a profound impact on Elvis, who often spoke of Jesse.

Isaac Newton:

Parliament Member: Newton served as a member of Parliament for the University of Cambridge. However, he's said to have spoken on the floor only once, asking for a window to be closed because he felt a draft.

Queen Victoria:

Photography Enthusiast: Queen Victoria was one of the first monarchs to have her photograph taken, and she became an avid supporter of photography, even using it to document her family life.

Pythagoras:

Mystical Beliefs: Apart from his famous theorem, Pythagoras believed in the transmigration of souls (reincarnation) and had a personal philosophy that included dietary restrictions; he and his followers were vegetarians influenced by religious beliefs.

Henry Ford:

Dancing: Ford was an avid dancer, particularly enjoying old-time dancing. He even installed a dance floor at his Highland Park plant for employees to use during breaks.

Mark Twain (Samuel Clemens):

Patent Holder: Twain held three patents, one for a self-pasting scrapbook, another for an improvement to suspenders, and a third for a history game.

Ernest Hemingway:

Polydactyl Cats: Hemingway had a love for cats, especially polydactyl cats (cats with extra toes). There's still a colony of these cats at his Key West home, which is now a museum.

Catherine the Great:

Cultural Patronage: While often remembered for her personal life, Catherine was a significant patron of the arts and sciences, expanding the Russian Academy of Sciences and collecting a vast array of art, some of which formed the Hermitage Museum.

Wolfgang Amadeus Mozart:

Child Star: Mozart was not just a prodigy but a child star in his time, composing music at five, performing for royalty by six, and writing his first symphony at eight.

Cleopatra:

Scholarly: Cleopatra was known for her intellectual pursuits, being fluent in multiple languages, including Egyptian, which was rare for the Ptolemaic rulers, and she was also a noted mathematician and chemist.

Julius Caesar:

Epilepsy: Caesar is believed to have suffered from epilepsy, known in his time as "the falling sickness." He was known to collapse during important events, which might have been epileptic seizures.

Michelangelo:

Anatomy Studies: To perfect his depiction of the human form, Michelangelo dissected corpses. He was granted special permission by the Catholic Church to study anatomy in this manner, which was otherwise forbidden.

Alexander the Great:

Immortalized Wine: After Alexander's death, his closest friend, Hephaestion, was said to have been buried with an eternal flame and an urn of Alexander's favorite wine, which was to be kept burning forever.

Jane Austen:

Secret Love: There's evidence to suggest that Austen had a romantic interest in a clergyman named Thomas Lefroy, though their relationship was cut short by family and financial considerations. She never married.

Leonardo da Vinci:

Vegetarianism: While not strictly a vegetarian, da Vinci was known for his compassion towards animals, often buying caged birds just to set them free. His notebooks contain passages where he argues against eating meat.

Marie Curie:

Family of Nobel Laureates: Marie Curie's daughter, Irène Joliot-Curie, also won a Nobel Prize in Chemistry, making them the first mother-daughter pair to win Nobels. Her husband, Pierre Curie, and her daughter's husband, Frédéric Joliot-Curie, are also Nobelists.

Charles Dickens:

Sleepwalking: Dickens was known to sleepwalk, often writing in his sleep, a fact that fascinated his biographer John Forster.

Rosa Parks:

Civil Rights Leader: Before her famous refusal to give up her bus seat, Parks was already an active member of the NAACP, fighting against racial segregation.

Albert Einstein:

Pacifist Views: Einstein was a committed pacifist, renouncing his German citizenship partly due to anti-war sentiments, until WWII, when he supported the Allies against the Nazis.

Benjamin Franklin:

Swimming Enthusiast: Franklin was an enthusiastic swimmer and even invented a pair of wooden hand paddles to aid swimming, which he wrote about in his autobiography.

Queen Victoria:

Mourning Period: After the death of her husband, Prince Albert, in 1861, Queen Victoria entered into a long period of mourning, wearing black for the rest of her life and known as the "Widow of Windsor."

Winston Churchill:

Painting for Peace: Churchill found peace in painting, which he took up in his 40s during a period of political exile. His paintings were often signed with an anchor, his symbol for hope.

Nikola Tesla:

Pigeon Love: Tesla had a peculiar attachment to pigeons, particularly one white dove with which he shared a deep emotional bond, claiming it was the only creature to have given him love.

Vincent van Gogh:

Ear Incident: The story that van Gogh cut off his entire ear is an exaggeration; he actually cut off a piece of his left earlobe, possibly as a gesture of reconciliation or in a moment of mental distress.

Mark Twain (Samuel Clemens):

Humor and Satire: Twain's biting humor was not just for entertainment; he was a critic of American society, targeting racism, imperialism, and other societal ills with his work.

Marie Antoinette:

Charity: Despite her reputation, Marie Antoinette was known for her charitable acts, particularly towards children and the poor, often giving away her own dresses and funds.

Thomas Edison:

Sleep Habits: Edison was known for his polyphasic sleep schedule, where he would take multiple short naps throughout the day rather than sleeping for long periods at night.

Cleopatra:

Linguistic Skills: She could allegedly speak up to nine languages, which was unusual for a Ptolemaic ruler, showcasing her intellectual engagement with her realm and beyond.

Pythagoras:

Dietary Restrictions: He and his followers adhered to a strict vegetarian diet, believing in the transmigration of souls and thus promoting non-violence towards all forms of life.

Boudicca:

Celtic Warrior Queen: Boudicca, the queen of the Iceni tribe, led a significant revolt against Roman rule in Britain around 60-61 AD. However, after her death, her legacy was largely forgotten until it was romanticized in the Victorian era.

Genghis Khan:

Genetic Legacy: Geneticists estimate that approximately 1 in 200 men alive today are direct descendants of Genghis Khan or his immediate male relatives, due to the extensive spread of his genetic lineage across Asia and Europe.

Unexpected Inventions

History is littered with inventions that were stumbled upon rather than meticulously planned. Here are some fascinating examples of such serendipitous discoveries:

The Microwave Oven:

Percy Spencer's Candy Bar: While working with radar equipment in 1945, Percy Spencer of Raytheon noticed that a chocolate bar in his pocket had melted due to the heat generated by the magnetron. This led to the development of the microwave oven, revolutionizing kitchen appliances.

Post-it Notes:

Low-Tack Adhesive: Spencer Silver, a scientist at 3M, was trying to create a super-strong adhesive but ended up with one that was only moderately sticky. It was Art Fry, another 3M scientist, who used this adhesive to keep his bookmark from falling out of his hymn book, leading to the invention of Post-it Notes.

Potato Chips:

Chef George Crum's Retaliation: In 1853, at Moon's Lake House in Saratoga Springs, New York, chef George Crum, irritated by a customer repeatedly sending back his fries for being too thick, decided to slice potatoes paper-thin and fry them until they were crisp. This accidental creation became the first batch of potato chips.

Slinky:

Richard James' Spring Coil: Naval engineer Richard James was working on stabilizing devices for instruments on ships when he knocked a spring off a shelf. Instead of falling straight down, it "walked" down rather than falling, which gave him the idea for the Slinky toy in 1943.

Penicillin:

Alexander Fleming's Moldy Dish: In 1928, after returning from a holiday, Alexander Fleming noticed that a mold (Penicillium notatum) growing in one of his petri dishes had killed off the surrounding bacteria. This observation led to the development of penicillin, the world's first antibiotic.

Corn Flakes:

Kellogg Brothers' Health Experiment: John Harvey Kellogg and his brother Will Keith were experimenting with different diets at the Battle Creek Sanitarium. They left some cooked wheat to sit, which resulted in it flaking. They toasted these flakes, creating what would become Corn Flakes, initially as a health food.

Teflon:

Roy Plunkett's Freon Experiment: In 1938, Roy Plunkett, a chemist at DuPont, was working on new refrigerants when he discovered that one of his experimental gases had polymerized into a white, waxy solid inside a refrigerated bottle. This substance, which was extremely slippery, was later developed into Teflon.

Super Glue:

Harry Coover's Monomer: While attempting to make clear plastic gun sights during WWII, Harry Coover and Fred Joyner found that cyanoacrylate, the compound they were working with, stuck to everything it touched. Initially dismissed, it was later realized this could be useful as an adhesive, leading to Super Glue.

The Pacemaker:

Wilson Greatbatch's Mistake: Greatbatch accidentally installed the wrong resistor into a circuit he was building to record heart sounds in 1956. Instead of recording, it produced an electrical pulse that mimicked the human heart, leading to the development of the implantable pacemaker.

Safety Glass:

Édouard Bénédictus' Broken Flask: In 1903, French chemist Édouard Bénédictus dropped a flask in his lab, expecting it to shatter completely. Instead, it held together due to a layer of plastic nitrate left inside from a previous experiment, inspiring safety glass for cars.

Vulcanized Rubber:

Charles Goodyear's Spilled Rubber: While experimenting with rubber to make it more durable, Charles Goodyear accidentally spilled a mix of rubber and sulfur onto a hot stove. The result was vulcanized rubber, which was more durable and less sensitive to temperature changes than natural rubber.

Velcro:

George de Mestral's Dog Walk: After a walk in the woods with his dog in 1941, George de Mestral was intrigued by the burrs that stuck to his clothes and his dog's fur. Examining them under a microscope, he noticed the hook-like structure and was inspired to create Velcro.

The Popsicle:

Frank Epperson's Frozen Drink: In 1905, 11-year-old Frank Epperson left a mixture of powdered soda and water with a wooden stirrer on his porch overnight. It froze, and he later realized he had accidentally invented what he called the "Epsicle," later renamed the Popsicle.

The Chocolate Chip Cookie:

Ruth Graves Wakefield's Shortage: In 1930, Ruth Graves Wakefield, the owner of the Toll House Inn, ran out of baker's chocolate while making cookies. She chopped up a Nestlé semi-sweet chocolate bar expecting it to melt and mix into the dough. Instead, the chocolate pieces held their shape, creating the first batch of chocolate chip cookies.

Play-Doh:

Wallpaper Cleaner to Child's Play: Originally invented in the 1930s as a wallpaper cleaner, Play-Doh was repurposed by the wife of one of the inventors for her kindergarten class. It became popular as a modeling compound for children when schools removed lead from their wallpaper.

Saccharin:

Taste of Artificial Sweetness: In 1879, Constantin Fahlberg, a chemist working at Johns Hopkins University, forgot to wash his hands after a day's work. While eating dinner, he noticed a sweet taste and traced it back to a chemical he had been working with, leading to the discovery of saccharin.

X-Rays:

Wilhelm Röntgen's Fluorescent Screen: While experimenting with cathode rays in 1895, Wilhelm Röntgen noticed that a screen coated with a fluorescent material began to glow even though it was not directly in the path of the cathode rays. This led to the discovery of X-rays.

The Frisbee:

Pie Tins in the Park: Students at Yale University in the late 19th century started throwing around empty pie tins from the Frisbie Pie Company. This playful activity inspired the modern Frisbee, patented by Walter Morrison in 1957, who initially called it the "Pluto Platter."

The Match:

John Walker's Accidental Flame: In 1826, John Walker, an English chemist, was stirring a mix of chemicals with a stick when he noticed that the dried lump at the end of the stick caught fire when scraped on the floor. This led to the invention of the friction match.

Coca-Cola:

John Pemberton's Headache Remedy: Originally concocted by John Pemberton in 1886 as a cure for headaches, Coca-Cola was initially made from coca leaves and kola nuts. It was intended as a patent medicine but became famous as a soft drink.

The Trampoline:

George Nissen and Larry Griswold's Tumbling: Inspired by trapeze artists' safety nets, George Nissen and Larry Griswold, both gymnasts, developed the trampoline in 1936 to help with tumbling exercises. They named it from the Spanish word "trampolín," meaning "diving board."

The Lava Lamp:

Edward Craven Walker's Egg Timer: Edward Craven Walker was inspired to create the lava lamp after watching a homemade egg timer made of a cocktail shaker at a pub. He wanted to create something that would mimic the movement of underwater lava flows.

The Sticky Note:

Art Fry's Bookmarking Issue: As mentioned, Art Fry from 3M discovered how to use Spencer Silver's low-tack adhesive to solve his frustration with bookmarks falling out of his hymnal. This resulted in the creation of Sticky Notes.

The Electric Guitar:

Les Paul's Experimentation: Les Paul, a musician, and inventor, was dissatisfied with the volume of acoustic guitars. He experimented by attaching a phonograph needle to a guitar, amplifying it through a radio speaker, leading to the development of the solid-body electric guitar.

The Microscope:

Antonie van Leeuwenhoek's Lens Grinding: In the late 17th century, Antonie van Leeuwenhoek, a Dutch tradesman with no scientific training, ground small lenses as a hobby. His curiosity led him to observe things like bacteria for the first time, effectively inventing microbiology.

The Pina Colada:

Ramón "Monchito" Marrero's Coconut Shortage: In 1954, Ramón Marrero, a bartender at the Caribe Hilton in Puerto Rico, was asked to create a new drink. Facing a coconut shortage, he used coconut cream instead of coconut milk, inventing the Piña Colada.

The Potato Head:

George Lerner's Vegetable Parts: Originally, George Lerner created Mr. Potato Head as a set of plastic, stickable parts for real vegetables. When the toy industry wasn't interested, he sold the idea to Hasbro, who decided to include a plastic potato body to avoid the mess of using real produce, turning it into the first toy advertised on television in 1952.

Froot Loops:

Kellogg's Colorful Mistake: Froot Loops were not originally intended to be multicolored. During a production mishap at Kellogg's, different batches of cereal came out with different colors. Instead of scrapping the batch, they marketed it as a fun feature, and it became a hit.

The First Postage Stamp:

Rowland Hill's Postal Reform: The Penny Black, the world's first adhesive postage stamp, came about somewhat serendipitously. Rowland Hill, who campaigned for postal reform in the UK, suggested prepayment of postage through stamps after noticing that letters were not being paid for by the recipient, leading to inefficiencies in delivery.

The Safety Pin:

Walter Hunt's Debt Solution: In 1849, Walter Hunt, a prolific but often cash-strapped inventor, created the safety pin from a piece of wire to pay off a $15 debt. He received patent number 6,281 for his design.

Bubble Wrap:

Alfred Fielding and Marc Chavannes' Wallpaper Experiment: While trying to create plastic wallpaper, Fielding and Chavannes accidentally invented bubble wrap in 1957. They initially marketed it as greenhouse insulation before it found its niche as protective packaging.

The Microwave Oven (Again, but with a twist):

Percy Spencer's Popcorn Incident: Following the melting candy bar incident, Percy Spencer also had a bag of popcorn kernels spill into the path of the magnetron, and they started popping. This further convinced him of the potential for microwave heating.

The Paper Clip:

Johan Vaaler's Paper Fastener: While looking for a simpler way to keep papers together, Norwegian inventor Johan Vaaler patented a design for a paper clip in 1899. Although simple, his design wasn't as practical as the now-familiar Gem clip introduced later without any patent.

The Band-Aid:

Earle Dickson's Concern for His Wife: Earle Dickson, a cotton buyer for Johnson & Johnson, invented the Band-Aid in 1920 because his wife often cut her fingers while cooking. He created a prototype by placing squares of cotton on strips of tape and covering them with crinoline to keep them sterile.

The Sphygmomanometer (Blood Pressure Cuff):

Scipione Riva-Rocci's Simple Solution: Scipione Riva-Rocci was attempting to measure blood pressure in the late 19th century. He found that by using a rubber cuff that could be inflated and placed around the arm, combined with a mercury manometer, he could measure systolic pressure effectively.

The Etch A Sketch:

André Cassagnes' Electrostatic Attraction: André Cassagnes, an electrician, accidentally discovered the principle behind the Etch A Sketch when a screen he was working on became electrostatically charged, allowing aluminum powder to stick to it. This led to the creation of what would become a beloved drawing toy.

The Pacemaker (another perspective):

Wilson Greatbatch's Circuit Misstep: As previously noted, Wilson Greatbatch's invention of the pacemaker came from installing the wrong resistor into his circuit. However, what's particularly interesting is that this mistake was made because he grabbed a 1-megohm resistor instead of a 10,000-ohm one, causing the circuit to produce a pulse similar to a heartbeat.

The Swiffer:

Procter & Gamble's Market Research: The Swiffer wasn't an accidental discovery, but its success came from an unexpected realization during market research. Procter & Gamble found that while consumers wanted an easy way to clean floors, they also wanted to avoid touching the dirt, leading to the development of disposable cleaning cloths on a stick.

The Chocolate Chip Cookie (another angle):

Ruth Wakefield's Intent: While Ruth did not intend to invent the chocolate chip cookie, her act of chopping up chocolate and mixing it into the dough was not a complete accident. She was looking for a way to add chocolate to cookies without melting it, but the result of the chocolate maintaining its shape was an unexpected success.

Chewing Gum:

Thomas Adams' Chicle Mistake: Thomas Adams was initially trying to use chicle, a sap from the sapodilla tree, as a rubber substitute. When that didn't work, he chewed on a piece and realized its potential as a chewable gum. Thus, modern chewing gum was born.

The Lemon Drop Candy:

George Herbert's Sour Innovation: George Herbert, a candy maker, accidentally dropped some sugar syrup into a lemon extract meant for flavoring. The result was a new kind of candy, the lemon drop, which became very popular.

Silicone:

J. Franklin Hyde's Shattered Dream: While trying to create a new type of glass, J. Franklin Hyde accidentally made silicone when he couldn't get the right formula for organic glass. This led to the versatile material used today in everything from cookware to medical devices.

The First Electric Washing Machine:

Alva J. Fisher's Housework Helper: In 1908, Alva J. Fisher's wife was frustrated with hand-washing clothes. Fisher, inspired by a hand-cranked machine, added an electric motor, creating the first electric washing machine, revolutionizing household chores.

The Ferris Wheel:

George Ferris' World's Fair Attraction: George Ferris was inspired to design his wheel after the Eiffel Tower's success at the Paris Exposition. He wanted to create something equally grand for the 1893 Chicago World's Fair, but the idea came to him as a way to outdo the Eiffel Tower, not from a direct need for amusement rides.

The Super Soaker:

Lonnie Johnson's Pressure Experiment: Lonnie Johnson, an engineer, was working on a heat pump prototype when he accidentally created a high-pressure water gun by connecting his device to a bathroom sink. This led to the invention of the Super Soaker in 1989.

The Breathalyzer:

Robert F. Borkenstein's Drunk Driving Solution: Borkenstein was looking for a reliable way to measure alcohol impairment. His invention came about when he realized that the same chemistry used for detecting carbon monoxide could be adapted to measure alcohol in breath.

The Popsicle (Once More):

Frank Epperson's Drink Mistake: Young Frank Epperson's accidental discovery of the Popsicle came when he left a mixture of soda water powder and water with a stirring stick on his porch overnight, and it froze. This was an accidental discovery, but it took years for him to realize its commercial potential.

The First Chocolate Bar:

Joseph Fry's Mixing Error: In 1847, Joseph Fry was experimenting with a blend of cocoa powder, cocoa butter, and sugar. When he accidentally mixed these ingredients smoothly enough to pour into a mold, he created the first solid chocolate bar.

The Fire Alarm System:

William F. Channing's Telegraphed Idea: While working on telegraph systems, William F. Channing realized that the same technology could be used to automatically alert people to fires. This led to the creation of the first fire alarm system.

The Potato Chip (Another Perspective):

George Crum's Frustrated Artistry: While often romanticized, George Crum's creation of the potato chip might also be seen as an act of frustration turned into innovation. His intention might have been sarcasm or annoyance, but the result was a culinary hit.

The Ice Cream Cone:

Italo Marchiony's Ice Cream Sandwich Alternative: Italo Marchiony, an Italian immigrant in the U.S., applied for a patent for an ice cream cone in 1903. However, a popular myth suggests that cones were invented during the 1904 St. Louis World's Fair when an ice cream vendor ran out of dishes and rolled up waffles into cones to serve ice cream.

Velcro (Another Look):

George de Mestral's Burdock Inspiration: George de Mestral's invention of Velcro was a deliberate attempt to mimic the way burdock burrs stick to fabric, but the observation itself was accidental. His curiosity about why burrs clung so effectively led to the development of Velcro.

CHAPTER 5

SCIENCE AND TECHNOLOGY

Breakthroughs that Changed Daily Life

The history of science and technology is paved with innovations that have fundamentally reshaped how we live, work, and interact with the world. Here are some key breakthroughs that have dramatically altered daily life:

The Internet:

Transformation: Initially a military and academic network, the public internet revolutionized communication, commerce, entertainment, and information access. It connects billions of people worldwide, making it an indispensable part of modern life.

Impact: From online shopping to remote work, from social media to streaming services, the internet has redefined social interactions, business models, and even our concept of privacy.

Electricity:

Invention: While not a single invention but a series of discoveries and developments, electricity has become the backbone of modern civilization.

Daily Use: It powers our homes, industries, and gadgets. The electric light bulb alone extended the day, allowing for night-time productivity and leisure. Refrigeration changed how we store and consume food, while electric motors and appliances reduced manual labor.

Automobiles:

Innovation: The internal combustion engine and the mass production techniques of Henry Ford made cars accessible to the masses.

Effect: Automobiles changed the landscape of cities, the nature of work commutes, and even our social norms, like dating. They've enabled suburban sprawl, altered trade logistics, and given rise to road trips and personal freedom of movement.

Penicillin:

Discovery: Alexander Fleming's accidental discovery of penicillin in 1928 ushered in the antibiotic age.

Life-Saving: This breakthrough transformed medicine by providing a tool to combat bacterial infections, drastically reducing mortality from diseases like pneumonia, syphilis, and even wounds from surgeries or battlefield injuries.

The Smartphone:

Evolution: From the first mobile phones to the sophisticated devices we carry today, smartphones combine computing power with portability.

Ubiquity: They've altered communication, navigation, entertainment, photography, and countless other aspects of daily life. They've made the world's knowledge, people, and services instantly accessible.

The Printing Press:

Johannes Gutenberg: His invention around 1440 made the mass production of books possible, which was pivotal in spreading knowledge during the Renaissance and Reformation.

Impact: It democratized learning, fueled the Scientific Revolution, and laid the groundwork for the modern era of mass communication and literacy.

Vaccines:

Edward Jenner's Work: The smallpox vaccine, and subsequently others, have saved countless lives by preventing once-deadly diseases from spreading.

Daily Life: Vaccinations have changed the trajectory of human health, allowing for safer childhoods, longer life expectancies, and the eradication or near-eradication of several diseases, fundamentally altering public health practices.

Air Conditioning:

Willis Carrier's Cooling: The invention of air conditioning in 1902 made living and working in hot climates comfortable year-round.

Influence: It has transformed urban development, enabling population growth in previously inhospitable areas, changed work habits, and even affected sleep patterns and productivity.

Semiconductors:

Transistor and Beyond: The invention of the transistor by William Shockley, John Bardeen, and Walter Brattain in 1947 led to the microchip, making electronics smaller, faster, and more powerful.

Technological Leap: Semiconductors are at the heart of computers, smartphones, and nearly all modern electronics, affecting every aspect of life from entertainment to medical devices.

Plastic:

Versatile Material: Leo Baekeland's invention of Bakelite in 1907 led to the plastic revolution, offering affordable, durable, and versatile materials.

Everyday Use: Plastics have changed everything from food packaging to medical equipment, influencing consumer culture, environmental concerns, and manufacturing processes.

GPS (Global Positioning System):

Satellite Navigation: Originally for military use, GPS became available for civilian use in the 1980s.

Impact: It has transformed navigation, logistics, agriculture, and even sports, making location-based services an integral part of daily life.

The Microwave Oven:

Accidental Invention: Percy Spencer's discovery led to a new way of cooking that saved time in food preparation.

Everyday Convenience: This has changed how we heat food, making meals quicker and influencing kitchen designs and meal planning.

The Pill (Oral Contraceptive):

Enovid: Introduced in the 1960s, the birth control pill gave women control over their reproductive choices.

Societal Change: It has had profound implications on family planning, career opportunities for women, and social dynamics.

Refrigeration:

Preservation: Carl von Linde's work on refrigeration systems in the late 19th century led to household refrigerators, changing how we store and consume food by extending shelf life and reducing waste.

Impact: It has allowed for longer supply chains in food distribution, enabled the growth of supermarkets, and altered dietary habits around the world.

The Assembly Line:

Henry Ford: The introduction of the assembly line for the Model T in 1913 drastically reduced the time and cost to produce cars.

Industrial Revolution: This method increased efficiency in manufacturing, affecting everything from car production to electronics, making goods more affordable and accessible.

The Transistor Radio:

Portable Electronics: The development of the transistor made portable electronics like the radio possible, revolutionizing how music, news, and entertainment were consumed on the go.

Cultural Impact: It played a significant role in the spread of music culture, especially rock 'n' roll, and provided a source of information during pivotal times like the Civil Rights Movement.

The ATM (Automated Teller Machine):

Banking Convenience: The ATM, first installed by Barclays in Enfield, London, in 1967, allowed people to access their funds outside of bank hours.

Effect: It changed banking habits, making financial transactions more convenient, and reduced the need for physical bank branches.

The Barcode:

Inventory Management: Introduced in supermarkets in the 1970s, the barcode has made checkout processes faster, inventory tracking more efficient, and supply chain logistics more manageable.

Consumer Impact: It has influenced pricing strategies, product tracking, and consumer behavior by enabling instant price comparisons and sales tracking.

Personal Computers:

Home Computing: The advent of affordable personal computers like the Apple II and IBM PC in the late 1970s and early 1980s brought computing power to homes and small businesses.

Daily Life: PCs have transformed education, work, entertainment, and communication, making digital literacy a necessity.

The Microscope:

Anton van Leeuwenhoek: While microscopes existed before, his improvements in lens crafting allowed for detailed observation of microorganisms.

Scientific Advancement: This tool has been pivotal in biology and medicine, leading to discoveries in microbiology, pathology, and countless health advancements.

The Green Revolution:

Norman Borlaug: His work in developing high-yield, disease-resistant wheat varieties dramatically increased food production.

Worldwide Effect: This revolution in agriculture saved billions from starvation, changed farming practices globally, and supported population growth by increasing food security.

Synthetic Fertilizers:

Haber-Bosch Process: Fritz Haber and Carl Bosch's process for synthesizing ammonia from nitrogen and hydrogen revolutionized agriculture by making nitrogen fertilizers widely available.

Agricultural Impact: It has been crucial in supporting the global population's food needs but also raised environmental concerns regarding pollution and soil degradation.

The Digital Camera:

Steven Sasson: At Eastman Kodak, he invented the first digital camera in 1975, although it took decades for digital photography to become mainstream.

Photography Revolution: Digital cameras have made photography accessible to everyone, changed how we capture and share memories, and disrupted the film industry.

Wireless Communication:

Guglielmo Marconi: His work on radio transmission laid the groundwork for all wireless communication technologies.

Ubiquity: From radio broadcasts to Wi-Fi and mobile networks, wireless technology has made information and connectivity ubiquitous, influencing everything from emergency services to social networking.

The Microwave Oven (Another Angle):

Time Efficiency: Beyond just reheating, microwave ovens have influenced cooking habits by speeding up the preparation of meals, especially for busy households.

Cultural Shift: It has led to changes in food consumption patterns, with a rise in convenience foods and quicker meal times.

DNA Fingerprinting:

Alec Jeffreys: His discovery in 1984 has had profound implications in forensic science, paternity testing, and even in wildlife conservation.

Legal and Social Impact: It has transformed legal systems by providing undeniable evidence in criminal cases and has helped in identifying remains, solving mysteries, and even exonerating the wrongly accused.

The Sewing Machine:

Isaac Singer: While not the first to invent a sewing machine, Singer's improvements and the introduction of the lockstitch mechanism made sewing machines practical for home use.

Impact: It revolutionized the clothing industry by speeding up production, lowering costs, and allowing for mass production of garments, which changed fashion and consumer habits.

The Dishwasher:

Josephine Cochrane: Invented in the late 19th century, her dishwasher was initially designed for large households and commercial use but eventually found its way into homes.

Daily Convenience: It has saved countless hours of manual labor, influenced kitchen design, and changed hygiene standards.

The X-Ray Machine:

Wilhelm Röntgen: His discovery of X-rays in 1895 led to a new era in medical diagnostics.

Health Care: X-rays have become a fundamental tool in medicine, allowing for non-invasive examination of the body, aiding in everything from setting broken bones to detecting diseases like cancer.

The Safety Razor:

King C. Gillette: His disposable blade safety razor made shaving safer and more accessible for the general public.

Cultural Change: This invention not only simplified personal grooming but also played a role in the evolution of hygiene practices and beauty standards.

The Zipper:

Whitcomb L. Judson: Although the modern zipper we know today was perfected by Gideon Sundback, Judson's initial hook-and-eye fastener was the precursor.

Practicality: Zippers have influenced fashion and clothing design, making it easier for people to dress and undress, impacting everything from shoes to luggage.

The Electric Vacuum Cleaner:

Hubert Cecil Booth: Developed the first powered vacuum cleaner in 1901, although it was initially a large, cumbersome machine.

Home Maintenance: This invention transformed household cleaning, making it less labor-intensive and improving indoor air quality.

The Elevator:

Elisha Otis: His safety elevator made vertical transportation safer, leading to the development of skyscrapers.

Urban Development: Elevators have changed cityscapes, allowing for high-rise buildings and influencing urban planning, real estate, and how we live in cities.

Anesthesia:

William Morton: The public demonstration of ether anesthesia in 1846 was a pivotal moment, allowing for painless surgery.

Medical Practice: This has transformed surgery into a much less traumatic experience, enabling more complex procedures and improving patient outcomes.

The Incandescent Light Bulb:

Thomas Edison: While not the sole inventor, Edison's work on a practical, long-lasting incandescent light bulb was a significant step towards modern lighting.

Lifestyle Change: It extended productivity hours, influenced entertainment, and altered sleep patterns by making artificial light widely available.

The Jet Engine:

Frank Whittle: His development of the jet engine in the 1930s led to faster air travel.

Global Connectivity: Jet travel has shrunk the world, making long-distance travel more accessible, influencing globalization, tourism, business, and even time zones with the advent of jet lag.

The Birth of the Digital Watch:

Hamilton Watch Company: Introduced the first digital watch in 1970, using LED technology.

Timekeeping: Digital watches have changed how we perceive and interact with time, making it more precise and accessible, impacting everything from sports to fashion.

The Refrigerator (Another Angle):

Freon: The introduction of Freon by Thomas Midgley Jr. in the 1930s made refrigeration systems safer and more efficient.

Food Industry: This not only changed household consumption but also the entire cold chain logistics, influencing global food distribution and preservation techniques.

The Calculator:

Early Models to Texas Instruments: From mechanical devices like Blaise Pascal's Pascaline to the handheld electronic calculators of the late 20th century.

Education and Business: Calculators have made complex calculations quicker and more accessible, affecting education, finance, engineering, and daily accounting.

The Telephone:

Alexander Graham Bell: His invention in 1876 transformed communication, allowing voices to be carried over long distances.

Social and Business Impact: It has been fundamental in shaping modern communication, leading to the development of telephone networks, call centers, and ultimately, the mobile phone revolution.

The Steam Engine:

James Watt: His improvements to the steam engine in the late 18th century greatly increased its efficiency, catalyzing the Industrial Revolution.

Economic and Social Impact: It transformed transportation, manufacturing, and agriculture, leading to urbanization, the expansion of railways, and the mechanization of industry.

The Telegraph:

Samuel Morse: His development of the Morse code and the practical telegraph system allowed for the first time near-instantaneous long-distance communication.

Communication Revolution: It laid the groundwork for the information age, influencing everything from news dissemination to the coordination of railway systems.

The Airplane:

Wright Brothers: Their first successful flight in 1903 marked the beginning of aviation.

Globalization: Air travel has connected the world like never before, affecting trade, tourism, military strategy, and personal travel, making the planet seem smaller.

The Radio:

Guglielmo Marconi: Although many contributed to its development, Marconi's work led to the widespread adoption of radio communication.

Entertainment and Information: Radio broadcasting transformed entertainment, news, and emergency communication, bringing a shared cultural experience into homes.

The Television:

John Logie Baird & Philo Farnsworth: Their pioneering work in the 1920s and 1930s on mechanical and electronic television systems, respectively.

Cultural Shift: Television has been a major influence on culture, politics, and socialization, offering visual storytelling and live broadcasts of events into living rooms worldwide.

The Modern Battery:

Voltaic Pile by Alessandro Volta: While batteries existed before, Volta's 1800 invention provided a reliable source of electricity.

Portable Power: This led to the development of portable devices, from early portable radios to modern smartphones, affecting how we consume media, communicate, and work on the go.

The Calculator (Continued Evolution):

Electronic Calculators: The miniaturization of electronics allowed for the creation of pocket calculators, democratizing mathematical computation.

Education and Commerce: They've made arithmetic instant and error-free, impacting education, business, and everyday decision-making.

The Personal Computer (Another Perspective):

Microprocessor Development: The Intel 4004 by Ted Hoff in 1971 was one of the first microprocessors, which made personal computing possible.

Information Age: Personal computers have changed how we work, learn, communicate, and entertain ourselves, leading to the digital revolution.

The World Wide Web:

Tim Berners-Lee: Invented in 1989 at CERN, the web provided a user-friendly way to access information over the internet.

Global Information Exchange: This has fundamentally altered how information is shared, how businesses operate, and how we interact socially, economically, and politically.

GPS (Another Angle):

Satellite Technology: The launch of the first Navstar GPS satellite in 1978 by the U.S. Department of Defense.

Navigation: Beyond basic navigation, GPS technology has applications in precision agriculture, time synchronization, and geofencing, among others.

The Microwave Oven (Additional Context):

Mass Production: Raytheon's Radarange was developed during WWII, but it was the countertop models of the 1960s that popularized microwave cooking.

Food Culture: This technology not only changed cooking habits but also influenced food preparation techniques, packaging, and even restaurant operations.

Polymerase Chain Reaction (PCR):

Kary Mullis: Developed in the 1980s, PCR allows for the amplification of DNA, making it possible to detect and analyze minute amounts of genetic material.

Biotechnology: It's crucial in fields like forensics, medical diagnostics, and genetic engineering, enabling personalized medicine and rapid disease identification.

The Windshield Wiper:

Mary Anderson: Patented in 1903, her invention made driving in inclement weather safer and more comfortable.

Automotive Safety: This device has become standard on vehicles, significantly improving visibility during rain or snow, thus enhancing safety.

These innovations have not only improved efficiency or convenience but have also had sweeping effects on culture, economy, environment, and personal lifestyle, showcasing the profound and often unintended consequences of technological advancement.

Lesser-Known Scientists and Their Contributions

Science is often celebrated through the achievements of iconic figures like Einstein or Newton, but many unsung heroes have made substantial contributions to our understanding of the world. Here are some lesser-known scientists whose work has had a profound impact:

Hedy Lamarr:

Frequency Hopping: An actress by trade, Lamarr was also an inventor who, along with composer George Antheil, developed a "Secret Communication System" during WWII. This technology used frequency hopping to prevent jamming of radio-guided torpedoes, laying the groundwork for modern wireless communications like Wi-Fi, Bluetooth, and GPS. Her contributions weren't widely recognized until much later.

Katherine Johnson:

NASA Calculations: Before the era of digital computers, Johnson's mathematical prowess helped calculate the trajectories for NASA's early space missions, including the Apollo 11 moon landing. Despite her critical role, her contributions were largely overlooked until recent times.

Emmy Noether:

Noether's Theorem: A pioneering mathematician, Noether's work on abstract algebra and theoretical physics led to Noether's Theorem, which relates symmetries in physics to conservation laws. Her influence on modern physics is immense, yet she faced significant gender discrimination during her career.

Barbara McClintock:

Jumping Genes: McClintock's discovery of genetic transposition, or "jumping genes," revolutionized our understanding of genetics. Although initially met with skepticism, her work was eventually recognized with a Nobel Prize in Physiology or Medicine in 1983.

Rachel Carson:

Environmental Awareness: Her book "Silent Spring" in 1962 sparked the modern environmental movement by highlighting the dangers of pesticides, particularly DDT. Carson's work in marine biology and her advocacy for environmental protection were revolutionary.

Lise Meitner:

Nuclear Fission: Despite her significant role in the discovery of nuclear fission, Meitner's contributions were often overshadowed by her male colleagues. She was instrumental in interpreting the results that led to the splitting of the atom, but she did not share in the Nobel Prize awarded to Otto Hahn for this discovery.

Percy Spencer:

Microwave Oven: As mentioned before, Spencer's accidental discovery of the heating effect of magnetrons led to the invention of the microwave oven. His work at Raytheon transformed kitchen design and food preparation globally.

Vera Rubin:

Dark Matter: Rubin's observations on the rotation of galaxies provided evidence for the existence of dark matter, a substance that makes up about 27% of the universe but cannot be seen directly. Her work was pivotal in cosmology, yet she did not receive a Nobel Prize.

John von Neumann:

Computer Architecture: His contributions to computer science include the von Neumann architecture, which describes how a computer processes instructions and data. He also worked in quantum mechanics, game theory, and economics, influencing fields from computing to nuclear strategy.

Ida Noddack:

Element Discovery: With her husband Walter Noddack, she discovered the element rhenium. Her suggestion that nuclear fission might involve the splitting of atomic nuclei predated Hahn and Strassmann's work but was initially dismissed.

Mary Anning:

Paleontology: Though not formally trained, Anning made significant contributions to paleontology by discovering numerous fossils from the Jurassic period, including the first ichthyosaur skeleton to be correctly identified.

Chien-Shiung Wu:

Parity Violation: Known as the "First Lady of Physics," Wu's experimental proof of the non-conservation of parity in weak nuclear interactions was groundbreaking. Her male colleagues received the Nobel for the theory she helped confirm, but she did not.

Eunice Newton Foote:

Greenhouse Effect: In 1856, Foote conducted experiments demonstrating that carbon dioxide could absorb heat, thereby contributing to the understanding of the greenhouse effect. Her work was presented at a scientific meeting but largely forgotten until rediscovered years later.

George Gamow:

Big Bang Theory: Gamow's work in nuclear physics, genetics, and cosmology included contributions to the Big Bang theory, though his student Ralph Alpher is more commonly cited for this due to a famous paper that included the names Alpher, Bethe, and Gamow for a playful pun on alpha, beta, gamma.

Gertrude B. Elion:

Pharmacology: Elion developed numerous drugs for treating diseases like leukemia, herpes, and preventing organ transplant rejection. Her work with George Hitchings led to a Nobel Prize in Physiology or Medicine in 1988.

Alice Ball:

Leprosy Treatment: She developed an injectable oil extract from the chaulmoogra tree, which was the most effective treatment for leprosy until sulfone drugs were introduced in the 1940s. Her work was continued by others after her untimely death.

Anita Roberts:

Transforming Growth Factor-beta (TGF-β): Her research on TGF-β revealed its role in cell growth, differentiation, and tissue repair, significantly impacting cancer research and treatments.

Dorothy Crowfoot Hodgkin:

X-ray Crystallography: Her work using X-ray crystallography to determine the structure of biomolecules like penicillin and insulin was groundbreaking. She won the Nobel Prize in Chemistry in 1964.

Rosalind Franklin:

DNA Structure: Her X-ray diffraction images of DNA, particularly Photo 51, were pivotal in determining the double helix structure of DNA. However, her role was overshadowed by Watson and Crick until later acknowledgments.

Harriet Brooks:

Radioactivity: A student of Ernest Rutherford, Brooks made significant contributions to the study of radioactivity, including discovering the nuclear transmutation of radon into polonium.

Reshma Kewalramani:

Medicine and Genetics: Her research has focused on the genetic basis of human diseases, contributing to the understanding of how genetic variations influence disease susceptibility.

Lynn Margulis:

Symbiotic Theory: She proposed the endosymbiotic theory, which explains how eukaryotic cells evolved through the incorporation of bacteria. This theory has become central to our understanding of cell biology.

Yvonne Brill:

Rocket Propulsion: Known for her work in improving rocket and jet propulsion, Brill developed a better way of controlling the fuel flow in rocket engines, significantly enhancing satellite propulsion systems.

Nettie Stevens:

Sex Determination: Stevens discovered sex chromosomes, identifying that sex is determined by the presence of X and Y chromosomes. Her work laid the foundation for modern genetics.

Otto Hahn (Beyond the Nobel):

While he's known for the discovery of nuclear fission, Hahn's contributions to radiochemistry, particularly in the discovery of protactinium and his work on nuclear isomers, are less recognized but significant.

Hertha Ayrton:

Electric Arcs: She made important contributions to the understanding of electric arcs and their use in electric lamps. Ayrton also invented a fan to disperse poison gas during WWI.

Jocelyn Bell Burnell:

Pulsars: As a graduate student, Bell Burnell discovered pulsars, but her supervisor Antony Hewish won the Nobel Prize for this discovery. Her work has been recognized with many other awards later in life.

Peter Mitchell:

Chemiosmotic Theory: His theory explained how ATP is synthesized in mitochondria, fundamentally changing our understanding of cellular energy processes. He received the Nobel Prize in Chemistry in 1978.

J. Presper Eckert and John Mauchly:

ENIAC: Though not entirely unknown, their role in developing ENIAC, one of the first general-purpose electronic digital computers, is sometimes overshadowed by the media attention given to others like von Neumann.

Mária Telkes:

Solar Energy: Known as "The Sun Queen," Telkes developed the first solar heating system for homes and worked on solar distillation, solar ovens, and other solar-powered gadgets, pioneering solar energy applications.

Mary Somerville:

Science Popularization: Her books translated and explained complex scientific concepts to the public, making science accessible to non-experts in the 19th century, earning her the nickname "Queen of Nineteenth Century Science."

Satyendra Nath Bose:

Quantum Statistics: Bose's work with Einstein on the statistics of photons led to the development of Bose-Einstein statistics, crucial for understanding systems of indistinguishable particles.

Williamina Fleming:

Astronomy: A "computer" at Harvard Observatory, she discovered the Horsehead Nebula, classified stars, and was instrumental in developing the Harvard Classification Scheme.

Futuristic Technologies That Exist Today

The future is here, with technologies that once existed only in science fiction now becoming part of our daily lives or showing immense potential for near-future applications. Here are some of the most intriguing futuristic technologies available today:

Quantum Computing:

Quantum Bits (Qubits): Unlike classical bits, qubits can exist in multiple states simultaneously due to superposition, allowing quantum computers to process information in ways that classical computers can't, potentially revolutionizing fields like cryptography, drug discovery, and climate modeling.

CRISPR-Cas9 Gene Editing:

Genetic Modification: This technology allows for precise, directed changes to the DNA of living organisms. Applications range from curing genetic diseases to creating genetically modified organisms with enhanced traits, raising both ethical questions and enormous potential for medicine and agriculture.

Artificial Intelligence (AI) and Machine Learning (ML):

Beyond Chatbots: AI now powers everything from autonomous vehicles to predictive analytics in healthcare. Machine learning algorithms are improving at a rapid pace, enabling systems to make decisions, recognize patterns, and even generate creative content with minimal human input.

Augmented Reality (AR) and Virtual Reality (VR):

Immersive Experiences: AR overlays digital information on the real world, used in applications like navigation, gaming, and education. VR creates entirely simulated environments for gaming, training, and virtual tourism, with applications in therapy, education, and remote work.

Brain-Computer Interfaces (BCI):

Direct Neural Control: Companies like Neuralink are working on BCIs that could allow users to control computers and other devices with their thoughts or restore capabilities to those with paralysis.

3D Printing:

From Prototyping to Production: Beyond models and prototypes, 3D printers now construct homes, produce complex medical implants, and even print food. This technology promises to revolutionize manufacturing, construction, and personalized medicine.

Lab-Grown Meat:

Cultured Meat: Scientists have successfully grown meat in labs using animal cells, offering a potential solution to ethical concerns about animal farming, reducing the environmental footprint of meat production, and potentially providing a more sustainable protein source.

Space Tourism:

Commercial Spaceflight: Companies like SpaceX, Blue Origin, and Virgin Galactic are making space travel for civilians a reality. While still in its infancy, this technology could soon allow tourists to experience space.

Hydrogen Fuel Cells:

Clean Energy: These cells convert hydrogen into electricity, producing only water as a byproduct, offering a clean alternative for vehicles and energy storage, potentially revolutionizing our approach to sustainable energy.

Flexible and Wearable Electronics:

Next-Generation Wearables: From e-textiles that can change color or generate electricity to flexible screens that can be rolled or folded, these technologies are paving the way for a future where electronics are part of our clothing and environment.

Graphene:

Miracle Material: With its incredible strength, conductivity, and flexibility, graphene is poised to transform everything from battery technology to water filtration, offering applications in electronics, energy, and environmental protection.

Invisibility Cloaks:

Metamaterials: While not true invisibility, researchers have created materials that can bend light around objects or absorb it, making them effectively invisible to certain wavelengths, with potential uses in military and optics.

Biometric Authentication:

Beyond Fingerprints: Now includes facial recognition, iris scanning, and even heartbeat patterns for secure authentication, making security both more personal and less intrusive.

Smart Cities Technology:

Urban Intelligence: Incorporating IoT, AI, and big data analytics to optimize everything from traffic flow and energy use to waste management, aiming for efficiency, sustainability, and improved quality of life.

Robotic Exoskeletons:

Assistive and Augmentative: These suits can assist with mobility for the disabled or enhance strength for workers, impacting rehabilitation, construction, and even military applications.

Digital Twins:

Virtual Models: Creating digital replicas of physical systems or processes for simulations, allowing for predictive maintenance, urban planning, and even personalized medicine by modeling patient-specific conditions.

Energy Harvesting:

Power from the Environment: Technologies that capture energy from ambient sources like movement, light, heat, or even radio waves, potentially powering wireless sensors and IoT devices indefinitely.

Neurotechnology for Mental Health:

Treating with Technology: Transcranial magnetic stimulation (TMS) and other neurotechnologies are being used to treat depression, anxiety, and other mental health issues without the side effects of medication.

Programmable Matter:

Shape-Shifting Materials: Imagine materials that can change their form, color, or properties on demand. Programmable matter, like digital materials that can self-assemble into different structures, could revolutionize manufacturing, robotics, and even clothing.

Optogenetics:

Light-Controlled Cells: This technology allows for the control of cells, particularly neurons, with light, offering potential breakthroughs in treating neurological disorders, understanding brain functions, and even creating bio-driven computing systems.

Personalized Medicine:

Tailored Therapies: Using genetic data and AI to design treatments specific to an individual's genetic makeup, improving efficacy and reducing side effects. This is becoming more prevalent with pharmacogenomics.

Quantum Internet:

Unhackable Networks: Leveraging quantum entanglement to create networks where information can't be copied or intercepted without detection, potentially revolutionizing secure communication.

Neural Dust:

Miniature Brain Sensors: Tiny, wireless sensors that can be sprinkled into the nervous system to monitor or stimulate neurons, potentially leading to new ways to diagnose and treat neurological conditions.

Bioprinting:

3D Printing Organs: Using bioinks made of living cells, this technology aims to print functional organs for transplantation, offering hope for patients needing organ replacements without the wait for donors.

Nano-robots:

Medical Nanobots: Researchers are developing nanoscale robots that could travel within the body to deliver drugs directly to cancer cells, clean arteries, or even repair tissue at a cellular level.

Memory Implants:

Restoring and Enhancing Memory: Early experiments aim at using implants to restore lost memories or enhance cognitive functions, with potential applications for Alzheimer's and other memory-related conditions.

Artificial Womb Technology:

ECTOLife Concept: Although still in conceptual stages, artificial wombs could one day be used to grow premature babies or even to extend pregnancy beyond the natural term, offering new possibilities in neonatal care.

Invisibility for Communication:

Invisible Wireless Signals: Using techniques like electromagnetic cloaking, researchers are working on ways to make wireless signals invisible to detection, which could have implications for privacy, security, and communication.

Haptic Feedback Technology:

Touch in Virtual Spaces: Advanced haptics are allowing for more realistic touch feedback in VR and gaming, but also in telepresence robotics for surgery or remote machinery control.

Energy Beaming:

Wireless Power Transfer: Technologies like laser power beaming or resonant inductive coupling are being explored to transmit energy over long distances, potentially changing how we distribute and use electricity.

Self-Healing Materials:

Autonomous Repair: Materials that can repair themselves when damaged, which could extend the life of everything from electronics to infrastructure, reducing maintenance costs and waste.

Swarm Robotics:

Collective Intelligence: Small robots working in large groups that can coordinate to perform tasks too complex or dangerous for a single robot, with applications in agriculture, disaster response, and exploration.

Mind Uploading:

Digital Consciousness: While still in theoretical stages, the concept involves transferring a person's mind into a digital form, potentially allowing for digital immortality or consciousness transfer.

Atmospheric Water Generators:

Hydrating from Air: Devices that extract water from humidity in the air, offering a solution for water scarcity in dry regions or survival situations.

AI-Driven Synthetic Biology:

Designing Life: AI is being used to design new biological entities, pathways, or even whole organisms, with applications in drug discovery, biofuel production, and environmental cleanup.

Terahertz Technology:

Beyond 5G: Terahertz waves for communication could provide data rates much higher than 5G, enabling ultra-fast, low-latency networks for future IoT, autonomous vehicles, and smart cities.

Quantum Sensors:

Precision Beyond: Using quantum properties to measure physical quantities with unprecedented accuracy, these could revolutionize fields like navigation, medical imaging, and environmental monitoring.

Privacy-Preserving AI:

Secure AI: Techniques like federated learning allow AI models to be trained across multiple decentralized devices or servers without exchanging data, enhancing privacy in machine learning applications.

Molecular Nanotechnology:

Atom-by-Atom Assembly: The vision here is to build materials and devices from the ground up, atom by atom. While still largely theoretical, some basic forms like nanoscale machines are being researched to potentially revolutionize manufacturing and medicine.

Zero-Energy Devices:

Self-Powered Electronics: Devices that can function without an external power source by harvesting ambient energy from their environment (light, heat, vibration), aimed at creating truly sustainable IoT ecosystems.

Artificial Photosynthesis:

Green Energy: Mimicking photosynthesis to convert carbon dioxide, water, and sunlight into energy or fuels, offering a sustainable energy solution that could also help in carbon capture.

Holographic Displays:

3D Without Glasses: True 3D displays that can project images into space without the need for special glasses, enhancing VR/AR experiences, medical imaging, and education.

Exascale Computing:

Supercomputing: Systems that can perform a quintillion (10^{18}) operations per second, enabling simulations of complex systems like the human brain, climate change, or new materials at an unprecedented scale.

Synthetic Blood:

Universal Blood Substitute: Efforts to create artificial blood that can be used in transfusions without the need for blood type matching, potentially saving millions in emergency situations.

Digital Twins for Human Health:

Your Health Modeled: Not just for infrastructure, digital twins are being developed for human beings, allowing for personalized simulations of how diseases might progress or how treatments might affect a specific individual.

Regenerative Medicine with Stem Cells:

Growing New Tissues: The use of stem cells to grow organs, repair damaged tissues, or treat degenerative diseases, moving towards a future where organ shortages are a thing of the past.

Smart Dust:

Microscopic Sensors: Tiny wireless sensors that can be distributed in the environment to collect data on anything from environmental conditions to structural integrity of buildings.

Quantum Batteries:

Charging in a Quantum Leap: Quantum mechanics might offer new ways to store and release energy more efficiently than traditional batteries, potentially revolutionizing energy storage.

Genetically Engineered Plant Factories:

Plants as Bioreactors: Plants engineered to produce pharmaceuticals, biofuels, or even plastics, turning agriculture into a platform for industrial production.

AI in Creativity and Art:

Machines as Artists: AI systems that can create original art, music, or literature, challenging our notions of creativity and opening new avenues in entertainment and design.

Privacy Enhancing Technologies (PETs):

Secure Data Sharing: Technologies designed to allow data to be used for analysis without revealing individual details, crucial for big data while protecting privacy.

Biological Computers:

DNA Computing: Using DNA to store data and perform calculations, offering massive storage capacity and parallel processing capabilities far beyond silicon-based computers.

Advanced Wearable Sensors:

Health Monitoring Skin: Wearables that go beyond devices to integrate into clothing or even directly onto the skin, monitoring health metrics continuously and seamlessly.

Insect-Sized Drones:

Micro Air Vehicles: Drones small enough to mimic insects, for uses in surveillance, pollination assistance, or even search and rescue operations in tight spaces.

Reversible Computing:

Energy-Efficient Data Processing: A theoretical approach to computing where no energy is wasted in computation, potentially leading to computers that don't heat up or consume much power.

AI with Emotional Intelligence:

Empathetic AI: Systems that can understand and respond to human emotions, impacting areas like mental health care, customer service, and personal assistance.

Underwater Drones:

Aquatic Exploration: Autonomous underwater vehicles for deep-sea exploration, environmental monitoring, and potentially for underwater construction or mining.

Augmented Human Abilities:

Cybernetic Enhancements: From exoskeletons to brain implants, technologies aimed at enhancing human physical or cognitive abilities, from soldiers to athletes to everyday people.

These technologies push the boundaries of what we consider possible, blending science with fiction to address some of humanity's greatest challenges while also presenting new ethical dilemmas and societal questions.

CHAPTER 6

ART AND CULTURE

Unique Traditions from Around the World

The tapestry of human culture is rich with traditions that are as varied as they are fascinating. These customs, rituals, and celebrations not only define communities but also offer a window into the values, history, and beliefs of different societies. Here are some unique traditions from various corners of the globe:

La Tomatina - Buñol, Spain:

Tomato Fight: Every last Wednesday of August, Buñol hosts what is arguably the world's largest food fight, where participants throw overripe tomatoes at each other, an event that began as a spontaneous act in 1945 and has since become a symbol of fun and unity.

Diwali - India:

Festival of Lights: Celebrated by millions of Hindus, Sikhs, and Jains worldwide, Diwali marks the victory of light over darkness. Homes are lit with diyas (clay lamps), fireworks light up the sky, and families exchange gifts, sweets, and celebrate with feasts.

The Day of the Dead (Día de los Muertos) - Mexico:

Honoring the Deceased: This celebration occurs on November 1st and 2nd, where families create altars with offerings to invite the spirits of the dead back for a reunion. It's a colorful festival filled with skulls, marigolds, and pan de muerto (bread of the dead).

The Cheese Rolling at Cooper's Hill - Gloucester, England:

Chase the Cheese: Participants chase a nine-pound wheel of Double Gloucester cheese down a steep hill. The winner, usually the first to reach the bottom or catch the cheese, keeps it as a prize. This event showcases a mix of tradition, sport, and local pride.

The Wife Carrying Championship - Finland:

Eukonkanto: Originating from a 19th-century legend, this competition sees men carrying their wives or partners through an obstacle course. The origins might be playful, but it's now an international event with teams from around the world.

Setsubun - Japan:

Bean-Throwing Ceremony: On February 3rd or 4th, to celebrate the coming of spring and ward off evil spirits, people throw roasted soybeans while chanting "Oni wa soto! Fuku wa uchi!" ("Demons out! Luck in!"). This tradition also includes eating the number of beans corresponding to one's age for good luck.

The Holi Festival - India and Nepal:

Festival of Colors: Holi marks the arrival of spring, the victory of good over evil, and the playful throwing of colored powders. It's a time when social norms are relaxed, and people from all walks of life come together in a vivid display of unity.

The Fiesta de San Fermín (Running of the Bulls) - Pamplona, Spain:

Encierro: Part of the San Fermín festival, this involves running in front of a small group of bulls that have been let loose on a course through the streets of Pamplona, culminating in bullfights. It's a tradition that dates back to the 13th century.

The Monkey Buffet Festival - Lopburi, Thailand:

For the Monkeys: In honor of the town's large population of macaque monkeys, Lopburi holds an annual feast where locals set out a lavish spread of fruits, vegetables, and sweets for the monkeys. It's part homage and part tourist attraction.

The Festival of the Giant Omelette - Bessières, France:

Omelette Géante: Commemorating the legend of Napoleon and his army being fed an omelette, the locals of Bessières cook an omelette made with around 15,000 eggs in a giant pan, symbolizing community and hospitality.

The Up Helly Aa - Shetland, Scotland:

Viking Fire Festival: Celebrating Shetland's Norse heritage, this event features torchlit processions, the burning of a Viking longship, and ends with community partying. It's one of Europe's largest fire festivals.

La Diablada - Oruro, Bolivia:

Dance of the Devils: Held during Carnival, it features elaborate costumes and dance performances where participants dress as devils and angels, representing the battle between good and evil, with roots in both Catholic and indigenous traditions.

The Kanamara Matsuri - Kawasaki, Japan:

Fertility Festival: Known as the "Festival of Steel Phallus," it's held at the Kanayama Shrine to pray for fertility, safe childbirth, and marital harmony. The festival features phallic-shaped candies, decorations, and even a mikoshi (portable shrine) carried in the parade.

The Highland Games - Scotland and Scottish Diaspora:

Strength and Skill: These games celebrate Scottish and Gaelic culture through events like the caber toss, where competitors toss a large wooden pole, along with traditional music, dance, and food.

The Boryeong Mud Festival - Boryeong, South Korea:

Mud Fun: Initially started to promote the cosmetic benefits of the local mud, this festival has grown into a massive event where people cover themselves in mud, play mud games, and enjoy mud-themed activities.

The Songkran Water Festival - Thailand:

New Year's Splash: During the Thai New Year, Songkran in mid-April, the streets become battlegrounds where everyone douses each other with water. It's a tradition meant to cleanse and renew, both literally and symbolically.

The Naadam Festival - Mongolia:

Three Manly Sports: This festival focuses on the three traditional Mongolian sports of wrestling, horse racing, and archery. It's a celebration of the country's nomadic heritage, where participants show off skills that were once essential for survival.

The Polar Bear Swim - Various Locations, Notably in Canada:

Freeze Dip: On New Year's Day, brave individuals plunge into icy waters, often dressed in festive costumes. It's seen as a way to start the year with vigor, cleanse the old, and embrace the new.

The Baby Jumping Festival (El Colacho) - Castrillo de Murcia, Spain:

Leap of Faith: In this centuries-old tradition, men dressed as devils jump over infants lying in the street to cleanse them of original sin, a practice unique to this small village.

The Night of the Radishes - Oaxaca, Mexico:

Noche de Rábanos: Held on December 23rd, artists carve intricate figures from large radishes to depict scenes from daily life, history, or religion. It's an ephemeral art form, as the radishes wilt quickly.

The Hornbill Festival - Nagaland, India:

Celebration of Tribes: This cultural festival showcases the traditions of the Naga tribes through dances, music, crafts, and sports like the bamboo pole climbing. It's an attempt to preserve and promote Naga heritage.

The Festival of Lanterns - Chiang Mai, Thailand:

Yi Peng: During this festival, thousands of handmade lanterns are released into the sky to symbolize the release of bad luck and the welcoming of good fortune. Coupled with Loy Krathong, where floating baskets are sent down rivers, it creates a spectacular sight.

The Burning of the Devils (Das Fasnacht) - Switzerland:

Fasnacht: In the early hours of Fasnacht, which marks the beginning of Lent, children in costumes parade through the streets with lanterns. Later, adults in grotesque masks participate in parades, playing drums and flutes, to scare away winter and evil spirits.

The Sechseläuten - Zurich, Switzerland:

Burning of the Böögg: A spring festival where a large snowman effigy filled with explosives is set ablaze. The time it takes for the head to explode is believed to predict the summer weather.

The Feast of the Black Nazarene - Manila, Philippines:

Devotional Procession: Millions of devotees participate in a barefoot procession, pulling a life-sized statue of Jesus Christ known as the Black Nazarene, seeking miracles and expressing their faith.

The Cooper's Hill Cheese-Rolling - Gloucester, England (Another Angle):

Cheese Pursuit: This event not only involves chasing a cheese wheel but is also notable for the number of injuries and the sheer spectacle of the event, drawing participants from around the world.

The Saint Lucia's Day - Sweden and other Scandinavian countries:

Ljus Lucia: Celebrating the light in the darkest time of the year, young girls dressed in white robes with a wreath of candles on their heads lead processions, singing traditional songs, symbolizing the return of light.

The Cheese Rolling and Wake - Stilton, England:

Different Cheese Tradition: In Stilton, instead of chasing after cheese, participants roll cheeses towards the church, a tradition believed to bring good fortune to the church's maintenance.

The Fire Festival of Las Fallas - Valencia, Spain:

Effigy Burning: Artists create large, intricate sculptures called "fallas," which are paraded through the streets and then burned in a grand finale. It's both a celebration of Saint Joseph and a critique of societal issues through satirical figures.

The Gion Matsuri - Kyoto, Japan:

Grand Parade: One of the most famous festivals in Japan, involving processions of traditional floats (yama and hoko), which are considered works of art and are accompanied by music and dance.

The Tinku Festival - Bolivian Andes:

Ritual Battles: During this pre-Columbian festival, indigenous communities engage in ritualistic fights to honor the Pachamama, the Earth Goddess, with the belief that the spilt blood will ensure fertile lands.

The Kumbh Mela - India:

Mass Pilgrimage: Occurring every 12 years at each of the four holy sites (Allahabad, Haridwar, Ujjain, and Nashik), it's the largest peaceful gathering in the world where millions of Hindus gather for purification rituals in the sacred rivers.

The Sónar Festival - Barcelona, Spain:

Avant-Garde Music: While not ancient, this festival has become a tradition for electronic music enthusiasts, showcasing cutting-edge music, art, and technology since 1994.

The Flying Fish Festival - Barbuda:

Heritage Celebration: This festival celebrates the island's heritage with flying fish dishes, music, cultural performances, and boat races, symbolizing the importance of fishing in local culture.

The Blót - Scandinavia:

Norse Pagan Sacrifices: Revived in modern times by neopagans, Blót involves ancient rites of offering to gods with food, drink, or sometimes blood sacrifices (now symbolic or with animals killed for food) to ensure good harvests and luck.

These traditions, from the deeply religious to the purely celebratory, from the ancient to the relatively modern, illustrate the multifaceted nature of human culture. They are not only a means of preserving history but also of creating new memories and strengthening communal bonds.

Bizarre or Forgotten Art Movements

The history of art is replete with movements that challenged the norms of their time, often pushing boundaries in ways that were considered bizarre, radical, or even forgotten by the mainstream art narrative. Here are some of these intriguing art movements:

Futurism:

Dynamic and Anti-Tradition: Originating in Italy in the early 20th century, Futurism glorified speed, technology, and violence, seeing the beauty in the modern industrial world. It aimed to free Italy from its past, advocating for the destruction of museums and libraries, and was later co-opted by Fascist ideologies.

Dada:

Art of Anti-Art: Born from the disillusionment of World War I, Dada was an anarchic movement that rejected the logic, reason, and aesthetic standards of contemporary art and culture. It embraced absurdity, with works like ready-mades by Marcel Duchamp, who presented everyday objects as art, like his famous urinal titled "Fountain."

Surrealism:

Exploring the Unconscious: While somewhat mainstream now, Surrealism was initially seen as bizarre for its dream-like imagery and logic-defying compositions. Artists like Salvador Dalí and René Magritte challenged viewers to look beyond the rational into the realm of the subconscious.

Vorticism:

British Modernism: This short-lived movement in the UK around 1914-1915 was influenced by Cubism but had its own aggressive, angular style. It celebrated the energy and violence of the modern world, with artists like Wyndham Lewis at its forefront.

Rayonism:

Russian Avant-Garde: A brief offshoot of Cubo-Futurism, Rayonism was developed by Mikhail Larionov and Natalia Goncharova. It attempted to depict the dynamic expansion of color rays emanating from objects, suggesting a fourth dimension, which was quite abstract for its time.

Incoherent Art:

Precursor to Dada: This playful movement from late 19th-century France focused on humor and absurdity in art, predating Dada. It featured nonsensical works and even exhibitions like one where visitors were encouraged to throw potatoes at the paintings.

Fluxus:

Art as Life: In the 1960s, Fluxus blurred the lines between art and life, advocating for a form of art that was anti-commercial, interdisciplinary, and often involved events or performances that were whimsical, like Yoko Ono's "Cut Piece," where she invited the audience to cut pieces of her clothing off with scissors.

Neo-Dada:

Reviving Dada's Spirit: In the post-World War II era, artists like Jasper Johns and Robert Rauschenberg in the U.S. brought back Dada's playful critique of art, using found objects and everyday materials in their works, challenging what could be considered as art.

Situationist International:

Art for Revolution: More a political than an art movement, the Situationists, led by figures like Guy Debord, used art to critique capitalism and consumer society, promoting ideas like détournement (the subversion of existing media) to create new meanings.

The Stuckists:

Anti-Conceptual Art: Formed in 1999 in opposition to the conceptual and installation art that dominated the British art scene, the Stuckists advocate for a return to figurative painting, with a manifesto that also critiques the art establishment.

Les Automatistes:

Unconscious Creation: A Canadian movement from the 1940s, Automatism involved creating art through automatic techniques, where artists like Paul-Émile Borduas aimed to let the subconscious dictate the work, bypassing conscious control.

Lettrism:

Beyond Meaning: Originating in France around the same time as Abstract Expressionism, Lettrism, founded by Isidore Isou, focused on letters and typography, moving towards abstract sound and visual poetry, challenging the semantic and syntactic structures of language.

GUTAI:

Japanese Avant-Garde: Post-WWII, the Gutai group in Japan focused on performance and interaction with materials in a way that was spontaneous and often destructive, emphasizing the act of creation over the finished product.

The Anti-Art Movement:

Art Against Itself: A term used for various artists and movements that critique or reject the notion of art. This includes actions like Gustav Metzger's Auto-Destructive Art, where works were designed to disintegrate over time.

The Black Mountain College Artists:

Experimental Art Education: Not a movement per se but a school that became a hotbed for experimental art practices, influencing movements like Abstract Expressionism and Fluxus. It was here that John Cage performed his famous "4'33"," where the music was the ambient sounds of the environment.

The Hairy Who:

Chicago's Quirky Art: Active in the 1960s, this group of Chicago artists created works characterized by grotesque, humorous, and often psychedelic imagery, reacting against the mainstream art world's seriousness.

The Dogme 95:

Film Movement: Though primarily a film movement, Dogme 95, with its strict rules to strip cinema back to its basics, shares the spirit of many radical art movements, aiming to purify film art from artificiality.

These movements, whether they lasted for decades or just a few years, have left their mark on the art world, often by challenging what art could be or mean. They remind us that art isn't just about beauty or representation but can serve as a critique, a playful experiment, or a radical departure from the accepted norms, influencing generations of artists to come.

Music Facts That Will Surprise You

Music, an art form that resonates with us on multiple levels, is full of surprising facts and stories that reveal the depth and breadth of its influence and innovation. Here are some music facts that might astonish you:

Mozart Outsold Modern Pop Stars:

In 2016, a box set commemorating the 225th anniversary of Wolfgang Amadeus Mozart's death outsold albums by contemporary artists like Beyoncé, Adele, and Drake. Each set contained 200 CDs, which significantly boosted his sales figures for that year.

Elvis Presley Never Wrote His Songs:

Despite being one of the most iconic figures in music history, Elvis wrote very little of his own music. His role was more that of a performer, interpreting songs written by others with his unique style.

The Beatles Couldn't Read Music:

None of The Beatles could read or write music notation. Their creation process was based on playing by ear, experimenting, and recording, relying on their innate musicality rather than formal training.

The Longest Song Ever Recorded:

"As Slow as Possible" by John Cage is being performed in Halberstadt, Germany, where the piece started in 2001 and is scheduled to end in 2640, making it a 639-year performance.

The Shortest Song Ever:

"You Suffer" by Napalm Death clocks in at just 1.316 seconds, setting the record for the shortest song ever recorded.

The 'Hallelujah' Chorus Was Originally in English:

Handel's "Messiah," which includes the famous "Hallelujah" chorus, was first performed with English lyrics, although Handel himself was German and wrote many operas in Italian.

David Bowie's Real Eyes:

David Bowie's iconic mismatched eyes were due to a condition called anisocoria, which resulted from a childhood injury. One pupil was permanently dilated, giving the illusion of different colored eyes.

The 'Macarena' Was Originally Political:

The song "Macarena" was inspired by a flamenco school in Venezuela and was initially a political campaign song for a local candidate, before it evolved into the dance hit we know.

The Most Covered Song in History:

"Yesterday" by The Beatles is believed to be the most covered song in history, with over 2,200 versions recorded by various artists.

Prince Played All 27 Instruments on His Debut Album:

On his 1978 debut album, "For You," Prince played every instrument, showcasing his multi-instrumental talents.

The First Rock and Roll Song:

Many credit "Rocket 88" by Jackie Brenston and his Delta Cats (actually Ike Turner's band) as one of the first rock and roll records, released in 1951, introducing the electric guitar distortion that would become a hallmark of the genre.

The 'Brown Note':

There's a myth about a musical note (around 7 Hz) that could supposedly cause involuntary bowel movements or nausea. While this has been studied, conclusive evidence for humans is lacking.

The 'Piano' Was Named for Its Dynamics:

The piano, short for pianoforte, gets its name from its ability to play soft (piano) and loud (forte) sounds, a dynamic range which was innovative for keyboard instruments at its invention.

The Oldest Known Musical Composition:

The "Seikilos Epitaph," found in Turkey, is the oldest surviving complete musical composition, dating back to the 1st century AD.

The Beatles' 'Taxman' Was About Real Taxes:

George Harrison wrote "Taxman" inspired by the high tax rates in the UK at the time, where the government took 95% of their earnings above a certain threshold.

The Origin of 'Jingle Bells':

"Jingle Bells" was written for Thanksgiving, not Christmas, by James Lord Pierpont in 1857. It only became associated with the latter holiday over time.

Mozart's Scatological Humor:

Wolfgang Amadeus Mozart included many references to bodily functions in his letters and even some of his compositions, showing a side of his personality rarely discussed.

The 'Jolene' and 'I Will Always Love You' Same-Day Write:

Dolly Parton wrote both of these iconic songs in one day, with "Jolene" being written first and "I Will Always Love You" later that day after business dealings with Porter Wagoner.

The 'National Anthem' for the USA:

"The Star-Spangled Banner" was written by Francis Scott Key in 1814 and wasn't officially adopted as the U.S. national anthem until 1931.

The First Music Video on MTV:

The first music video shown on MTV was "Video Killed the Radio Star" by The Buggles on August 1, 1981.

Music on Mars:

NASA's Curiosity rover played a song on Mars in 2012, using its drill to "chime" out "Happy Birthday" for itself, marking one year on the Martian surface.

The Silent Record:

In 1950, avant-garde artist John Cage composed "4'33"," a piece consisting of four minutes and thirty-three seconds of silence, challenging listeners to consider ambient sounds as music.

The First Hip-Hop Record:

"Rapper's Delight" by The Sugarhill Gang, released in 1979, is often credited as the first hip-hop record to gain widespread commercial success, although the genre began in the 1970s with DJ Kool Herc.

Classical Music in Warfare:

During World War II, the British used classical music as psychological warfare, playing it over loudspeakers to disrupt the sleep and morale of the German troops.

The 'Stairway to Heaven' Copyright Case:

In one of the most famous copyright cases, Led Zeppelin was accused of plagiarizing the opening riff of "Stairway to Heaven" from the band Spirit's "Taurus," but they were eventually cleared in 2016, though the debate continues among fans and legal experts.

The 'Milli Vanilli' Scandal:

The duo Milli Vanilli won a Grammy for Best New Artist in 1990 but had to return it after it was revealed they did not sing on their album; they lip-synced to tracks sung by other vocalists.

The Beatles Stopped Touring in 1966:

After their last concert at Candlestick Park in San Francisco on August 29, 1966, The Beatles ceased touring due to the overwhelming noise from fans making live performance nearly inaudible, and John Lennon's controversial "more popular than Jesus" remark.

Reggae's International Hit:

Bob Marley's "No Woman, No Cry" was not his first song to gain international attention, but it's often credited with bringing reggae music to a global audience when it was released in 1974.

The 'Greatest Songwriter':

According to a poll by Rolling Stone magazine, Paul McCartney was voted the greatest songwriter of all time, narrowly beating out Bob Dylan.

The First Album to Be Digitally Recorded:

The 1976 album "Something/Anything?" by Todd Rundgren is often cited as the first rock album to be recorded directly to digital.

Electric Guitar Patent:

The first electric guitar was patented in 1937 by George Beauchamp and Adolph Rickenbacker, leading to the creation of the Rickenbacker guitar company.

The 'Surfin' USA' Controversy:

Chuck Berry's "Sweet Little Sixteen" was the basis for The Beach Boys' "Surfin' USA," leading to a lawsuit where Berry was credited as the song's writer in 1963.

The 'Most Valuable Album':

The Beatles' White Album, specifically Ringo Starr's personal copy with his annotations, sold for $790,000 in 2015, making it one of the most expensive records ever sold at auction.

The Origin of 'Rock Around the Clock':

Bill Haley & His Comets' "Rock Around the Clock" is often considered the first rock 'n' roll song to top the charts, but it was initially the B-side to another song, "Thirteen Women (and Only One Man in Town)."

The Longest Billboard Chart Run:

"The Twist" by Chubby Checker has the distinction of being the only song to reach number one on the Billboard charts twice, in 1960 and again in 1962.

The 'Unsinkable' Titanic Song:

"Nearer, My God, to Thee" was reportedly played by the band on the Titanic as it sank, but what song was actually played has been debated, with some survivors claiming it was "Autumn."

The First Music Played in Space:

In 1971, the crew of Apollo 15 played the song "I Was Born About Ten Thousand Years Ago" with a small guitar, making it the first music performance in space.

The World's Loudest Band:

The Guinness World Record for the loudest band ever is held by Manowar, who achieved a sound level of 129.5 decibels at a concert in 1994.

The 'Dark Side of the Moon' and 'The Wizard of Oz':

There's an urban legend that Pink Floyd's "The Dark Side of the Moon" album syncs up with "The Wizard of Oz" if you start the album at the third roar of the MGM lion, though both Floyd members and the film's creators deny any intentional connection.

'Happy Birthday' Copyright Issues:

"Happy Birthday to You" was under copyright for nearly a century, with Warner/Chappell Music claiming rights until a 2015 lawsuit deemed the copyright invalid, making it part of the public domain.

The 'MMMBop' Songwriters:

The Hanson brothers wrote "MMMBop" when they were around 12 to 15 years old, but their ages during the song's peak in 1997 were often misreported, leading to a misconception about their youth.

These facts illustrate how music intertwines with history, technology, legal battles, and cultural phenomena, often in ways that are as surprising as they are enlightening.

CHAPTER 7

SPACE FACTS

Oddities About Planets in Our Solar System

Our solar system is a treasure trove of oddities, each planet offering unique characteristics that challenge our understanding of cosmic environments. Here are some fascinating and lesser-known facts about the planets:

Mercury:

- **Extreme Temperatures**: Mercury has the most extreme temperature swings of any planet in the solar system due to its lack of atmosphere. Daytime temperatures can soar above 400°C (750°F), while at night they can plummet to -173°C (-279°F).

- **Shrinking**: The planet is shrinking. As it cools, Mercury's crust contracts, causing wrinkles on its surface known as lobate scarps. This process has reduced its diameter by about 7 kilometers over billions of years.

- **Hollows**: Mercury features mysterious geological formations called "hollows" - shallow depressions with bright interiors, possibly formed by the sublimation of volatiles from the surface material.

Venus:

- **Retrograde Rotation**: Venus rotates on its axis in the opposite direction to most planets, including Earth. This means the Sun rises in the west and sets in the east. Additionally, a day on Venus (one complete rotation) lasts longer than its year (time to orbit the Sun).

- **Runaway Greenhouse Effect**: The surface of Venus is hotter than Mercury's, despite being further from the Sun, due to a runaway greenhouse effect. Its atmosphere traps heat, making surface temperatures around 460°C (860°F).

- **Volcanic Activity**: Venus has more volcanoes than any other planet in the solar system, with over 1,600 major volcanoes. Some of these might still be active, but the thick clouds make it hard to observe directly.

- **Slow Rotation**: Venus takes about 243 Earth days to complete one rotation, which is longer than its year (224.7 Earth days to orbit the Sun), making its day longer than its year.

Earth:

- **The Blue Marble**: Earth is the only planet known to support life, thanks to a unique combination of water, atmosphere, and stable climate. Its nickname, "The Blue Marble," comes from its appearance from space, dominated by oceans.

- **Magnetic Field**: Earth has a strong magnetic field, generated by the movement of molten iron in its outer core. This field protects life from solar and cosmic radiation but is not perfectly aligned with the planet's rotation axis, leading to the South Magnetic Pole being in the Northern Hemisphere geographically.

- **Plate Tectonics**: Earth is unique for its active plate tectonics, where the crust is broken into plates that move, collide, and slide past each other, creating mountains, earthquakes, and volcanoes.

- **Moon's Unique Tilt**: Earth's Moon is tidally locked, always showing the same face to us. Interestingly, the Moon's orbit around Earth is tilted about 5 degrees relative to Earth's orbit around the Sun, affecting solar and lunar eclipses.

Mars:

- **Olympus Mons**: Mars hosts the largest volcano and mountain in the solar system, Olympus Mons, which is 13.6 miles (22 kilometers) high and 374 miles (600 kilometers) in diameter, roughly the size of Arizona.

- **Water and Life Debate**: Mars has water in the form of ice at its poles and possibly beneath its surface. The presence of methane in its atmosphere has fueled debates about potential life, past or present.

- **Methane Cycles**: Methane levels on Mars fluctuate, which could be due to geological processes or biological activity. This has led to speculation about life forms or geological methane vents.

- **Phobos and Deimos**: Mars's moons are so small and close that they rise and set twice a day. Phobos orbits so close to Mars that it appears to move backward in the sky.

Jupiter:

- **Great Red Spot**: This storm on Jupiter is a massive anticyclone that has been raging for at least 300 years, possibly much longer. It's so large that three Earths could fit inside it, though it has been shrinking in recent years.
- **Magnetic Field**: Jupiter's magnetic field is 20,000 times stronger than Earth's, creating intense radiation belts around the planet, which could be lethal to humans without significant protection.
- **Three Rings**: While less famous than Saturn's, Jupiter also has a ring system, composed mostly of dust from its moons, especially Adrastea and Metis.
- **Io's Volcanic Activity**: Jupiter's moon Io is the most volcanically active body in the solar system, with hundreds of active volcanoes due to tidal heating caused by Jupiter's gravity.

Saturn:

- **Hexagonal Storm**: At Saturn's north pole, there's a six-sided jet stream, a hexagonal storm system that's larger than Earth, with each side of the hexagon being about 13,800 kilometers long.
- **Density**: Saturn is the least dense planet in our solar system; if you could somehow place it in a bathtub large enough, it would float due to its composition being primarily hydrogen and helium.
- **Methane Rain on Titan**: Saturn's largest moon, Titan, has lakes, rivers, and seas of liquid methane and ethane, with rain cycles similar to Earth but with methane instead of water.
- **Shepherd Moons**: Saturn's rings are kept in shape by "shepherd moons," small moons like Prometheus and Pandora that affect the particles in the rings, keeping them confined.

Uranus:

- **Sideways Spin**: Uranus spins on its side, with an axial tilt of about 98 degrees. This might be due to a massive impact early in its history. Its poles experience 42 years of continuous sunlight followed by 42 years of darkness due to its long orbit around the Sun.

- **Cold but Bright**: Despite being the seventh planet from the Sun, Uranus has an extremely cold atmosphere, dropping to -224°C (-371°F), but it's unusually bright because its atmosphere reflects a lot of sunlight.

- **Magnetic Weirdness**: Uranus's magnetic field is tilted at 59 degrees from its axis of rotation and offset from the planet's center, making it unique in the solar system. This creates an unusual magnetosphere.

- **Seasonal Extremes**: Due to its extreme axial tilt, when Uranus has a season, it lasts for 21 years. During part of its year, one pole faces the Sun continuously while the other is in darkness.

Neptune:

- **Super Strong Winds**: Neptune has the strongest winds in the solar system, with speeds reaching up to 1,300 mph (2,092 km/h), due to its atmosphere's composition and temperature differences.

- **Dark Spots**: Similar to Jupiter's Great Red Spot, Neptune has dark spots, but they are not as long-lasting. These are thought to be large, rotating storm systems, with the first one discovered being the Great Dark Spot, observed by Voyager 2 in 1989.

- **Dark Spots and Storms**: The Great Dark Spot observed by Voyager 2 in 1989 had disappeared by 1994 when Hubble looked for it, showing how dynamic Neptune's atmosphere is. New dark spots have been observed since.

- **Triton's Retrograde Orbit**: Neptune's largest moon, Triton, orbits in the opposite direction to Neptune's rotation, suggesting it was captured rather than formed in situ. It also has geysers that eject nitrogen gas and dust particles.

Pluto (Dwarf Planet):

- **Heart-Shaped Feature**: Pluto has a large, heart-shaped nitrogen ice glacier named Tombaugh Regio after its discoverer, Clyde Tombaugh. This feature is about 1,000 miles (1,600 kilometers) across.

- **Atmosphere Changes**: Pluto's thin atmosphere, mainly nitrogen, collapses into its surface ice as it moves away from the Sun in its elliptical orbit, being absent or extremely thin during parts of its year.

- **Charon's Influence**: Pluto and its largest moon, Charon, are so close in size that they orbit a point outside Pluto itself, making Pluto-Charon a binary system rather than a planet with its moon.

- **Surface Age**: Despite being far from the Sun, parts of Pluto's surface are surprisingly young, with features like Sputnik Planitia, likely kept smooth by the convective turnover of nitrogen ice.

Miscellaneous Solar System Oddities:

- **The Kuiper Belt**: Beyond Neptune, the solar system hosts a region called the Kuiper Belt, full of icy bodies, dwarf planets like Pluto, and is thought to be the source of short-period comets.

- **Trojans**: Planets like Jupiter and Neptune have swarms of asteroids in their Lagrange points, called Trojans, which share the planet's orbit around the Sun.

- **Interstellar Objects**: While not planets, our solar system has been visited by interstellar objects like 'Oumuamua, which was the first known object from another star system to pass through ours, highlighting how interconnected the galaxy might be.

These oddities not only highlight the diversity of planetary environments but also underscore the dynamic and sometimes bizarre processes at work in our solar system. Each planet's unique traits offer clues to its history, evolution, and the forces that shape it, continuing to captivate scientists and enthusiasts alike.

RARE AND UNUSUAL KNOWLEDGE

Strange Astronomical Events

The cosmos is full of events that defy our everyday understanding of physics and space, showcasing the universe's vast and often bizarre nature. Here are some of the most intriguing and unusual astronomical phenomena:

Tabby's Star (KIC 8462852):

This star, also known as Boyajian's Star, has exhibited irregular and extremely deep dips in brightness, far beyond what planets could cause. Theories range from a Dyson Swarm to comet clouds or interstellar dust, but no definitive explanation has been confirmed.

Fast Radio Bursts (FRBs):

FRBs are incredibly brief, powerful pulses of radio emission from unknown sources far beyond our galaxy. Their origin remains one of astronomy's biggest mysteries, with possibilities including merging neutron stars, black holes, or even extraterrestrial signals.

Supernova Impostors:

These are stars that suddenly brighten to rival supernovae in luminosity but don't explode. Instead, they might be experiencing a violent outburst or mass loss, misleading observers into thinking a star has gone supernova.

Quasar J0529-4351:

Discovered to be the brightest known object in the universe, it's powered by a supermassive black hole consuming material at a phenomenal rate. Its brightness is so intense that it outshines our Sun by 500 trillion times.

The Methuselah Star (HD 140283):

This star in the constellation Libra has an estimated age that, at one point, was thought to be older than the universe itself, presenting a paradox for astronomers. Recent, more accurate measurements have resolved this issue, but its status as one of the oldest stars remains.

Gamma-Ray Bursts (GRBs):

These are the most energetic electromagnetic events known to occur in the universe, typically associated with the death of very massive stars or the merging of neutron stars. They can outshine entire galaxies for brief moments.

The Disappearance of V838 Monocerotis:

After an outburst in 2002 that made it one of the largest known stars, V838 Monocerotis faded in brightness. Its light echo, however, provided astronomers with a unique opportunity to study the surrounding interstellar medium.

Oumuamua:

The first known interstellar object to pass through our solar system, 'Oumuamua's shape, speed, and trajectory have puzzled scientists. It was initially thought to be a comet, but showed no cometary activity. Hypotheses now range from a naturally occurring object to an alien spacecraft.

The Great Dimming of Betelgeuse:

In late 2019 to early 2020, Betelgeuse, a red supergiant in the constellation Orion, dimmed significantly, leading to speculation about an imminent supernova. It has since brightened, but the event remains a topic of study regarding the star's behavior.

The Cold Spot:

A region in the cosmic microwave background (CMB) radiation where the temperature is unusually low, dubbed the "Cold Spot." Its size and depth are larger than what the standard model of cosmology predicts, suggesting possibly unknown cosmic structures or phenomena.

Galactic Cannibalism:

When one galaxy merges with or consumes another, these events can dramatically affect the structure of the involved galaxies. An example is the Milky Way's ongoing consumption of the Sagittarius Dwarf Elliptical Galaxy.

Planetary Nebula Shapes:

Some planetary nebulae exhibit incredibly bizarre shapes, like the Butterfly Nebula or the Ring Nebula, formed by the interaction of stellar winds and radiation with the nebula's gas, creating intricate and beautiful designs.

The Boomerang Nebula:

This nebula is one of the coldest places in the universe, with a temperature of about 1 Kelvin (-272.15°C or -457.87°F), colder than the cosmic background radiation due to its rapid expansion.

Hypernova (GRB 190114C):

A hypernova, or superluminous supernova, is an extremely energetic explosion that releases two to eight times more energy than a regular supernova. GRB 190114C was the brightest gamma-ray burst ever recorded, showing that stars can produce even more violent deaths than previously imagined.

The Impossible Solar System of HD 106906:

This system features a massive planet that orbits its stars at an extreme distance, 650 times farther than Earth orbits the Sun. Such a setup challenges our understanding of how planets form and maintain their orbits.

The Antikythera Mechanism of the Cosmos:

Like an ancient celestial computer, there are cosmic structures like the "fossil" cosmic web where ancient galaxies cluster in ways that suggest the universe's structure at a much earlier phase, offering a view into the past.

The 'Lyman-Alpha Blob':

These are enormous clouds of hydrogen gas that emit Lyman-alpha radiation, some of which are among the largest objects in the universe and might be precursors to galaxy formation.

The Great Eruption of Eta Carinae:

In the 1840s, this star system underwent a massive eruption, temporarily becoming one of the brightest stars in the night sky, leaving behind the Homunculus Nebula, a bipolar nebula with intricate structures.

The Wow! Signal:

Detected in 1977 by the Big Ear radio telescope, this was a strong narrowband radio signal that lasted for about 72 seconds. Its source has never been identified, making it one of the most famous potential signs of extraterrestrial intelligence.

The Supervoid:

This is an unusually large region of the universe that contains significantly fewer galaxies than average. It's associated with the aforementioned Cold Spot in the cosmic microwave background, possibly indicating a region where the universe expanded faster than normal.

The Sh2-308 Nebula:

This nebula, shaped like a cosmic bubble, was formed when a fast-moving star plowed through the interstellar medium, creating a visual that looks eerily like a giant eye staring back at us from space.

The Trappist-1 Exoplanets:

The discovery of seven Earth-sized planets orbiting the ultracool dwarf star TRAPPIST-1 is remarkable. What's even stranger is that these planets might be in synchronous rotation with their star, meaning they always show the same face to it, creating permanent day and night sides.

The Double Quasar:

Known as QSO 0957+561, this is actually one quasar whose light has been bent by a galaxy in between it and us, creating the illusion of two quasars. This gravitational lensing effect allows us to study both the quasar and the intervening galaxy.

The Great Attractor:

An area of space towards which the Milky Way, along with hundreds of thousands of other galaxies, is being drawn by an unseen gravitational force. The exact nature of what lies there remains a mystery due to our view being obscured by the Zone of Avoidance.

The Magnetar:

These are neutron stars with extremely strong magnetic fields, stronger than any known in the universe. When a magnetar's magnetic field changes, it can emit bursts of gamma rays or suddenly slow down, events known as giant flares or glitches.

The Eye of Sauron Nebula (Henize 3-401):

This planetary nebula, named due to its striking resemblance to the Eye from "The Lord of the Rings," showcases the dramatic aftermath of a star's death with its symmetrical, glowing structure.

The Cosmic Hand:

MSH 15-52, a pulsar wind nebula, looks like a giant cosmic hand reaching out into space, created by a neutron star's wind interacting with the remnants of a supernova explosion.

The Pulsar in the Crab Nebula:

This pulsar is the collapsed core of the star that exploded as a supernova in 1054 AD. It rotates 30 times per second, emitting beams of radiation like a cosmic lighthouse, but it's also ejecting high-speed winds that sculpt the nebula around it.

The Dark Flow:

Astronomers have observed galaxy clusters moving in a specific direction at a very high speed, suggesting they could be influenced by something beyond the observable universe, perhaps hinting at multiverse theories.

The Runaway Star HD 148937:

This star is moving so fast that it's leaving its own stellar wind behind, creating a bow shock in the interstellar medium, which looks like a cosmic arrowhead pointing in the direction of its travel.

The X-Ray Chimneys of the Milky Way:

Fermi bubbles are two enormous structures extending above and below the Milky Way's center, possibly caused by the release of energy from either ancient supermassive black hole activity or star formation bursts.

The Cosmic Microwave Background (CMB) Anomalies:

Beyond the Cold Spot, there are other unusual features in the CMB like the alignment of certain temperature fluctuations that don't fit the standard model, suggesting there might be physics beyond what we currently understand.

The 'Impossible' Planet:

Kepler-78b is a planet so close to its star that it should not exist; given its proximity, it should have been engulfed or evaporated long ago, yet it persists, challenging our theories about planetary formation and survival.

The Star That Shouldn't Be There:

PSR J1719-1438b, a planet orbiting a pulsar, is a diamond planet, composed mostly of carbon in the form of diamonds, due to the extreme conditions under which it formed.

The Mystery of the Missing Baryons:

There's a discrepancy between the amount of baryonic (ordinary) matter predicted by Big Bang theory and what we can observe. Astronomers have been searching for these "missing baryons," potentially hidden in intergalactic filaments or within galaxy halos.

Space Travel Myths and Realities

Space travel has captured the human imagination for decades, leading to a mix of myths and misconceptions alongside the realities of venturing beyond Earth's atmosphere. Here's an exploration of some common myths juxtaposed with the actual facts:

Myth 1: The Great Wall of China is Visible from Space

Reality: This is one of the most enduring myths. From low Earth orbit, the Great Wall is not visible to the naked eye. Astronauts have reported that cities, roads, and even natural features like rivers and deserts are more visible.

Myth 2: There's No Gravity in Space

Reality: Gravity exists everywhere in space, but its effects diminish with distance. Inside spacecraft, occupants experience microgravity because both the craft and its contents are in free fall around Earth or another celestial body. However, astronauts still have mass and feel the gravitational pull towards the nearest large object, like Earth.

Myth 3: Space is Completely Silent

Reality: While there is no air in space to carry sound waves, space isn't silent. Electromagnetic vibrations, solar winds, and other phenomena can be translated into sounds by instruments, and inside spacecraft where there's air, sounds can still occur.

Myth 4: The Moon Landing Was Faked

Reality: Despite conspiracy theories, all evidence supports that the Apollo missions did indeed land on the Moon. There are thousands of pieces of physical evidence, including moon rocks, photographic evidence, and the fact that other countries' space probes have taken pictures of the landing sites.

Myth 5: You Can See Stars Easily During the Day from Space

Reality: Contrary to popular belief, seeing stars from space during the day isn't straightforward. The glare from the Sun and reflections off of spacecraft surfaces can make it difficult for astronauts to see stars without specialized equipment, much like on Earth.

Myth 6: You Would Explode if Exposed to Space

Reality: Exposure to the vacuum of space would be fatal, but not due to explosion. Without protection, bodily fluids would boil due to the lack of pressure, leading to unconsciousness within 15 seconds due to lack of oxygen, but the human body is tough enough to hold together.

Myth 7: Space Travel is Routine and Safe

Reality: While space travel has become more frequent, it remains inherently dangerous. The risks include radiation exposure, spacecraft malfunctions, and the isolation of long-duration missions. Each mission requires meticulous planning and safety measures.

Myth 8: Astronauts are Weightless in Space

Reality: They are in a state of microgravity, not weightlessness. Everything in the spacecraft, including the astronauts, is falling towards Earth at the same speed, creating the sensation of weightlessness.

Myth 9: The Space Shuttle Could Fly in Space Like an Airplane

Reality: The Space Shuttle was not designed for flying in space like an airplane; it was more like a "flying brick" that needed to be maneuvered with thrusters. Its ability to glide during re-entry was its most airplane-like feature.

Myth 10: Space Launches Are Environmentally Friendly

Reality: Current rocket technologies, especially those using liquid fuels, can have significant environmental impacts, including the release of pollutants into the atmosphere. There's ongoing research into more sustainable methods for space travel.

Myth 11: You Can Age Backwards in Space

Reality: While time does pass differently in space due to relativity (clocks on GPS satellites run slower than those on Earth), astronauts don't age backwards. They might experience time dilation where they age slightly less than someone on Earth, but this effect is minimal over the course of a human lifetime.

Myth 12: Mars Missions Are Just Around the Corner

Reality: While there are plans and aspirations for Mars missions, the challenges of sending humans to Mars and back safely are immense. These include radiation exposure, psychological effects of isolation, and life support for long durations. Mars missions are complex and still in the planning stages.

Myth 13: Space Tourism is Widely Accessible

Reality: As of now, space tourism remains an exclusive and expensive venture. While companies like SpaceX, Blue Origin, and Virgin Galactic are making strides, the cost remains prohibitive for the average person, and safety regulations are still being developed.

Myth 14: The Van Allen Radiation Belts Prevent Space Travel

Reality: These belts do contain high levels of radiation, but spacecraft can pass through them relatively quickly, minimizing exposure. Space agencies design missions to avoid prolonged stays in these belts, and spacecraft have protective measures against radiation.

Myth 15: Space Travel is Unaffected by Earth Politics

Reality: Space travel, particularly when involving international collaborations like the ISS, is deeply entwined with politics, international relations, and even national pride, affecting everything from funding to mission priorities.

Myth 16: You Can't Cry in Space

Reality: Astronauts can cry in space, but tears don't flow down their cheeks due to microgravity. Instead, they form into small floating balls. This can make the experience quite different from crying on Earth.

Myth 17: A Space Suit is Airtight

Reality: Space suits aren't completely airtight in the sense of being sealed against all pressure changes. They are designed to maintain a pressure differential between the inside and the vacuum of space but include mechanisms for pressure equalization to prevent the suit from bursting.

Myth 18: You Can Bounce on the Moon Like on a Trampoline

Reality: While gravity on the Moon is about one-sixth that of Earth, allowing for higher jumps, bouncing like on a trampoline isn't practical. Movement requires careful control to avoid injury, and astronauts use a hopping motion for locomotion.

Myth 19: Space Travel is the Biggest Contributor to the Spread of Alien Life

Reality: Current space missions are designed to be extremely cautious about cross-contamination. Protocols like NASA's Planetary Protection aim to prevent both forward contamination (Earth organisms polluting other worlds) and back contamination (alien organisms returning to Earth).

Myth 20: Water is a Rare Commodity in Space

Reality: Water is actually quite abundant in space but not in its liquid form. Comets, some moons, and even asteroids can contain water in the form of ice. The challenge is accessing and managing this resource for space travel.

Myth 21: Spacecraft Can Travel Faster than Light (FTL)

Reality: According to our current understanding of physics, nothing can travel faster than light. While there are theoretical concepts like wormholes or the Alcubierre Drive for FTL travel, they remain purely theoretical with significant challenges to overcome.

Myth 22: There's No Need for Hygiene in Space

Reality: Hygiene is critically important in space. Without regular showers (due to water conservation), astronauts use waterless cleaning methods like wet wipes. Hair and skin hygiene are managed to prevent clogs in the spacecraft's air filters and for the health of the crew.

Myth 23: Space Food is Dehydrated and Flavorless

Reality: While dehydrated and freeze-dried foods are used to save weight and space, modern space food has come a long way. Astronauts have a variety of meals including fresh fruits, vegetables, and even specially packaged hot meals. Food preservation technology has improved, and meal quality, flavor, and variety are considerations in space missions.

Myth 24: Space Suits are Designed for Combat

Reality: Although popular in science fiction, space suits are not armored for combat. They are primarily designed for protection against vacuum, extreme temperatures, and radiation, with mobility and life support being key features rather than combat readiness.

Myth 25: You Can Die from a Small Hole in a Spacecraft

Reality: A small hole or leak would not immediately cause death. Modern spacecraft have systems to detect and seal minor leaks. However, if left unaddressed, a significant depressurization event could be fatal over time due to oxygen loss and the inability to maintain internal pressure.

Myth 26: Earth's Orbit is Crowded with Space Junk Making Travel Hazardous

Reality: While space debris is a significant concern and can pose risks, especially in low Earth orbit, space is vast. Collisions are rare due to tracking and avoidance maneuvers. Efforts are being made to clean up orbit and mitigate future debris.

Myth 27: All Spacecraft Must Have a Human Crew

Reality: Unmanned or robotic spacecraft are extensively used for missions where human life is at risk, like to Venus, Mercury, or deep space explorations. These missions can be more cost-effective and allow for longer durations without the need for life support.

Myth 28: Space Travel Causes Bones to Disintegrate

Reality: While microgravity leads to bone density loss due to reduced calcium use (similar to osteoporosis), bones do not disintegrate. Astronauts engage in rigorous exercise routines to counteract this effect, and upon return to Earth, bone density can largely recover.

Myth 29: The Space Station Orbits Earth in a Perfect Circle

Reality: The International Space Station (ISS) actually follows an elliptical orbit, not a perfect circle, due to various gravitational influences and the need to adjust its path for various operational reasons.

Myth 30: You Can't Use Fire in Space

Reality: Fire behaves differently in space due to microgravity, but it can still exist. Combustion experiments have been conducted aboard the ISS, where flames form into spheres rather than the typical teardrop shape on Earth. Fire safety remains a crucial aspect of spacecraft design.

Myth 31: Spacecraft Must Always Land Vertically

Reality: Not all spacecraft land vertically. Some, like the Space Shuttle, were designed to glide and land on a runway horizontally. Others, like the Russian Soyuz, use parachutes and then land on land or water in a more traditional manner.

Myth 32: The Entire Spacecraft Burns Up Upon Re-entry

Reality: While parts of a spacecraft do burn up due to the intense heat of re-entry, the design of re-entry vehicles includes heat shields and ablative materials that protect the structure. The crew capsule or re-entry module, in particular, is built to withstand this heat and safely return to Earth.

Myth 33: You Can Easily Get Lost in Space

Reality: Space navigation is highly advanced, with spacecraft equipped with precise instruments like star trackers, GPS when near Earth, and Doppler radar for planetary landings. Getting "lost" in the traditional sense is not a concern; spacecraft have exact trajectories planned and followed.

Myth 34: Space Travel is Always Expensive

Reality: While traditional space missions are indeed costly, technological advancements and initiatives like SpaceX's reusable rockets are dramatically reducing the cost of access to space. Additionally, smaller satellite technologies and innovative launch methods are making space more affordable.

Myth 35: Spacecraft are Immune to Weather Conditions

Reality: Weather, particularly for launches, plays a significant role. Lightning, high winds, and storms can delay or cancel launches. Even in space, solar weather can affect spacecraft operations, with solar flares and coronal mass ejections posing threats to electronics and astronaut health.

Myth 36: All Spacecraft Travel in Straight Lines

Reality: Spacecraft often follow curved or elliptical orbits due to gravitational forces. They use maneuvers like Hohmann transfers for efficient travel between orbits or to reach other planets, which involves changing orbits rather than traveling in a straight line.

Myth 37: There's No Need for Restrooms in Space

Reality: Spacecraft are equipped with facilities for waste management. The International Space Station uses a vacuum toilet system, which is quite different from Earth toilets due to the need to manage waste in microgravity.

Myth 38: Food in Space is Only Consumed Through Tubes

Reality: While tubes were used in the early days of space travel, today's space food includes a variety of forms, from rehydratable meals to fresh fruits and vegetables. Astronauts have a variety of eating utensils and can consume food in forms similar to those on Earth, though adapted for space conditions.

Myth 39: Spacecraft Can Hover in Space

Reality: There's no 'hovering' in space as there's no atmosphere to provide lift or friction. Spacecraft either orbit around a body due to gravity or move in a straight line if they've escaped the gravitational influence of any body.

Myth 40: Astronauts Can Easily Walk in Space

Reality: Extra-Vehicular Activity (EVA) or spacewalks require extensive training and are physically demanding. Astronauts must be tethered to the spacecraft or station to prevent drifting away. Movement is slow and deliberate, using handholds and foot restraints due to the vacuum of space and microgravity.

Myth 41: Aliens Would Recognize Our Spacecraft

Reality: The design of human spacecraft is very much a product of our technology and engineering solutions. There's no guarantee that an alien civilization, if it exists, would recognize or understand our spacecraft designs as being for space travel.

Myth 42: Spacecraft Can Hide Behind Planets or Moons

Reality: While spacecraft can use planets or moons for gravitational slingshots or to block line-of-sight communications from Earth, the concept of hiding like in movies is impractical. The physics of orbital mechanics means their paths are predictable unless they use significant propulsion to alter their orbit.

Myth 43: Space Travel Doesn't Affect the Human Body

Reality: Long-duration space travel has several effects on the human body, including muscle and bone density loss, fluid redistribution causing "puffy face", changes in eyesight due to pressure on the optic nerve, and psychological impacts from isolation and confinement.

Myth 44: Space Is a Vacuum, So There's No Vibration or Noise

Reality: Inside spacecraft, there can be vibrations and noise from machinery, life support systems, and even the movement of crew members. Outside, while sound doesn't travel, vibrations from impacts by micrometeoroids or during docking maneuvers can be felt.

Myth 45: You Can Drink Alcohol in Space

Reality: Alcohol is generally not part of the diet in space due to health, safety, and regulatory reasons. However, in theory, astronauts could drink alcohol, but the effects in microgravity could be unpredictable and potentially hazardous.

These myths and realities illustrate the complexities and the realities of human space exploration, highlighting the advancements we've made while acknowledging the unique challenges space presents.

CHAPTER 8

COSMIC CONONDRUMS

Theories About the Universe's End

The ultimate fate of our universe has been a subject of fascination, speculation, and rigorous scientific inquiry. Here are some of the prominent theories about how it might all come to an end:

The Big Freeze or Heat Death (Entropy Maximum):

Theory: This scenario, also known as the "Big Chill" or "Heat Death," predicts that the universe will continue to expand indefinitely. As it does, stars will burn through their fuel, galaxies will move away from each other, and the universe will cool down to a state of maximum entropy.

Implications: Over time, new star formation will cease, galaxies will dim and die, black holes will eventually evaporate via Hawking radiation, and all matter will disperse. The universe will reach a state of thermal equilibrium where no energy can be used to perform work, leading to a static, cold, and dark universe.

The Big Rip:

Theory: If the expansion of the universe is driven by dark energy with a density that increases over time, the rate of expansion could become so rapid that it overcomes the binding forces holding together galaxies, stars, planets, and even atoms.

Implications: The "Big Rip" would see space itself being torn apart, leading to the disintegration of all structures in the universe. This would happen when the expansion rate exceeds the speed of light, which is theoretically possible if dark energy's strength grows without bound.

The Big Crunch:

Theory: If the density of the universe is high enough (or if gravity were to somehow become stronger than the force of expansion), the universe could stop expanding and begin to contract. This contraction would lead to a reversal of the Big Bang, where all matter collapses back into an infinitely hot, dense point.

Implications: Following the Big Crunch, there could be a "Big Bounce" where another universe starts expanding from the singularity, potentially leading to an endless cycle of universes. However, current observations suggest our universe's expansion is accelerating, making this scenario less likely.

The Big Slurp (Vacuum Metastability Event):

Theory: If our universe is in a false vacuum state, there's a possibility that a bubble of true vacuum could form and expand at the speed of light, converting the false vacuum into a lower-energy state. This would release an enormous amount of energy.

Implications: Everything within this expanding bubble would be annihilated or radically altered, potentially leading to a new form of universe with different physical laws. However, this theory depends on our current vacuum state being metastable rather than stable.

The Big Bounce:

Theory: This is an extension of the Big Crunch theory where the universe undergoes cycles of expansion (Big Bang) followed by contraction (Big Crunch), leading to a bounce or a new expansion phase without needing a singularity.

Implications: It suggests that our universe might be one in an infinite series of universes, each one possibly with different physical constants or laws. This avoids the singularity problem of the Big Bang but requires modifications to our current understanding of gravity and thermodynamics.

The Black Hole Era:

Theory: In this scenario, after the star formation era, all that remains are black holes of various sizes. As the universe expands, these black holes will eventually evaporate through Hawking radiation, but this process could take an unimaginably long time, leaving the universe dominated by black holes for most of its existence.

Implications: After black holes evaporate, what's left would be a scattering of elementary particles in a vast, cold expanse, leading to a final state similar to the Big Freeze.

Quantum Immortality or Eternal Inflation:

Theory: Based on the idea of eternal inflation, parts of the universe could continuously expand while other regions collapse, creating an infinite number of bubble universes. Quantum mechanics might also suggest that in one of these universes, life or consciousness persists indefinitely due to quantum effects.

Implications: This theory suggests that our observable universe might be just one in an infinite multiverse, where the end of one universe could be the beginning or continuation of another.

Each of these theories provides a different perspective on what could happen, influenced by our current understanding of physics, cosmology, and the nature of time and space. The end of the universe remains one of the most profound mysteries, with each theory offering a glimpse into the cosmic possibilities that await us or our descendants in the distant future.

The Concept of Time in Space

The concept of time in space challenges our everyday understanding, influenced profoundly by the theories of relativity:

Time Dilation:

Special Relativity: Albert Einstein's theory posits that time will dilate or slow down for an object in motion relative to an observer. The faster an object moves, the slower time passes for it. This effect becomes significant at speeds close to that of light. For example, astronauts on the International Space Station (ISS) experience time dilation due to their high orbital velocity; they age slightly less compared to someone on Earth over the same period.

General Relativity: Gravity also affects time. Clocks run slower in stronger gravitational fields, a phenomenon known as gravitational time dilation. Near massive bodies like neutron stars or black holes, this effect can be extreme. Time would pass much slower for an observer near a black hole's event horizon compared to someone far away.

Time as a Dimension:

In Einstein's model, time is treated as the fourth dimension, interlinked with the three spatial dimensions in what we call spacetime. This means that traveling through space also involves traveling through time; acceleration or deceleration can change an object's path through time.

Cosmic Time:

The age of the universe is estimated to be about 13.8 billion years. This "cosmic time" refers to the time elapsed since the Big Bang as observed from Earth. However, due to the universe's expansion, the light we see from distant galaxies shows them as they were in the past, effectively looking back in time.

Time in Different Frame of References:

Different observers in different gravitational fields or moving at different velocities can experience time differently. This leads to scenarios where what is simultaneous for one observer might not be for another, affecting communication and coordination in space travel.

Interstellar Travel and Time:

For long-duration space missions, especially to stars or beyond our solar system, time dilation could mean that travelers would age less than their counterparts on Earth. Upon returning, they might find that significantly more time has passed on Earth than during their journey, a concept popularized in science fiction but grounded in real physics.

Time Travel:

While time travel into the future is theoretically possible through high-speed travel or residing near massive objects like black holes, the concept of traveling backwards in time remains speculative. Theories like wormholes suggest pathways through spacetime that could theoretically allow for backward time travel, but these remain in the realm of theoretical physics.

Synchronization Issues:

Space agencies must account for time dilation effects when coordinating missions. For instance, GPS satellites must correct for both special and general relativistic effects to provide accurate positioning data.

Biological Time:

Humans and all life forms have internal clocks that are tuned to Earth's 24-hour day. In space, without natural day-night cycles, maintaining a daily rhythm requires artificial light cycles to prevent health issues from circadian rhythm disruption.

Philosophical Implications:

The relativity of time in space raises profound philosophical questions about the nature of time, causality, and the human experience of time as linear. It suggests that what we perceive as the arrow of time might be more flexible than we typically assume.

The study of time in the cosmos not only enhances our understanding of the universe but also shapes how we approach space exploration, interstellar travel, and even our theoretical grasp of the universe's history and future. It's a reminder that time, much like space, is not an absolute but part of a dynamic fabric where our place and motion within it influence our experience of reality.

Alien Life Speculation

The search for extraterrestrial life encapsulates some of the most profound questions humanity faces about our place in the universe. Here are various speculations on alien life:

The Drake Equation:

Proposed by Frank Drake in 1961, this equation attempts to estimate the number of active, communicative extraterrestrial civilizations in the Milky Way. It involves factors like the rate of star formation, the fraction of stars with planets, the number of planets that could support life, and the likelihood of civilization development. The equation's speculative nature invites both optimism and skepticism regarding alien life.

Habitable Zones:

The Goldilocks Zone: This concept suggests that life as we know it could exist on planets located in a star's habitable zone, where conditions might allow for liquid water. Speculation extends beyond this, considering various forms of life that might exist in environments we consider inhospitable.

Extremophiles: The discovery of extremophiles on Earth—organisms thriving in extreme conditions like high radiation, acidity, or temperature—fuels speculation that life could exist in extreme environments elsewhere in the universe.

Technosignatures:

Beyond biosignatures (signs of life like atmospheric gases), scientists speculate about technosignatures—indications of advanced technology. This could include radio signals, light pollution from cities, or even megastructures like Dyson spheres designed to harness a star's energy.

The Fermi Paradox:

Enrico Fermi famously asked, "Where is everybody?" if the universe is filled with life. This paradox highlights the contradiction between the high probability of extraterrestrial civilizations and the lack of evidence for, or contact with, such civilizations. Speculations to resolve this include:

- **The Rare Earth Hypothesis**: Suggests that Earth-like conditions necessary for complex life are very rare.
- **The Zoo Hypothesis**: Aliens might be observing us without revealing themselves, perhaps to avoid interfering with our development.
- **Civilizations are Short-Lived**: Advanced societies might destroy themselves before making contact.

The Search for Intelligent Life:

SETI (Search for Extraterrestrial Intelligence): This organization and others like it listen for radio signals or any electromagnetic emissions that could indicate intelligent life. The Wow! signal of 1977 is often cited as a potential technosignature, though its origin remains unexplained.

Alternative Biochemistries:

Speculation isn't limited to carbon-based life. Scientists ponder life forms based on silicon, or even life that uses different solvents like ammonia or methane instead of water, potentially existing on planets or moons with vastly different conditions from Earth.

Multiverse Theories:

Some speculate that if the universe is just one in an infinite multiverse, each with different physical laws, there could be an uncountable number of alien civilizations, each adapted to their unique cosmic environments.

The Great Filter:

This theory suggests that there might be a barrier or set of barriers in the development of intelligent life that makes it very rare. It could be at any stage from the formation of life to the point where civilizations become space-faring.

Life in Our Solar System:

Speculation about life in our solar system focuses on places like Mars, Europa (Jupiter's moon with a subsurface ocean), Enceladus (Saturn's moon with similar features), and Titan (which has lakes of methane and ethane). The search for microbial life or past evidence of life here is ongoing.

Alien Life and Consciousness:

Beyond physical life, there's speculation about consciousness or intelligence that might not be biological, possibly existing in forms we can't yet comprehend, like digital or energy-based lifeforms.

Interstellar Archeology:

If advanced civilizations have come and gone, there might be artifacts or ruins left behind for us to find, leading to a form of "archaeology" across the cosmos.

The speculation about alien life spans from the scientific to the philosophical, from the physical to the metaphysical. It touches on our deepest desires for connection, our fears of insignificance, and our curiosity about the nature of life and intelligence. Each new discovery in astrobiology, each technological leap in our ability to observe distant worlds, adds layers to these speculations, keeping the question of "Are we alone?" both open and endlessly fascinating.

CHAPTER 9

FOOD AND DRINK

Origins of Common Foods

Tracing the origins of common foods involves delving into history, archaeology, and anthropology. Here's an exploration of how some everyday foods came to be:

1. Pizza:

Origin: The precursor to pizza, flatbreads with toppings, has been enjoyed across many ancient civilizations. However, what we recognize as pizza today likely originated in Naples, Italy, in the late 18th or early 19th century. The famous Margherita pizza, named after Queen Margherita of Italy, was created in 1889 to reflect the Italian flag's colors with tomatoes, mozzarella, and basil.

2. Potatoes:

Origin: Potatoes are native to the Andes region of South America. They were first domesticated by the Inca Indians around 8,000 BC to 5,000 BC. Introduced to Europe by Spanish explorers in the 16th century, they didn't become a staple until much later, after overcoming initial suspicion and resistance.

3. Chocolate:

Origin: Chocolate originates from the cacao tree, which is native to the tropical regions of Central and South America. The Mayans and Aztecs were among the first civilizations to turn cacao seeds into a drink, considering it a food for the gods. Chocolate didn't become popular in Europe until the Spanish brought it back from the New World, where sugar was added to create the sweet treat we know today.

4. Sushi:

Origin: Sushi's history begins in Southeast Asia, particularly in what is now Thailand and Vietnam, where fish was fermented with rice to preserve it. This practice, called "narezushi," eventually evolved into "nigiri-zushi" in Japan, where the rice became part of the dish rather than just a fermenting agent. This evolution occurred around the 19th century.

5. Coffee:

Origin: Coffee's story begins in Ethiopia around the 9th century. Legend has it that a goat herder named Kaldi discovered coffee when his goats became more energetic after eating coffee cherries. From Ethiopia, coffee spread to the Arabian Peninsula and then globally, with the coffee plant being cultivated in regions like Yemen before spreading through trade routes.

6. Corn (Maize):

Origin: Corn, or maize, was first domesticated by indigenous peoples in Mexico about 10,000 years ago. It was a staple in the diet of civilizations like the Maya, Aztec, and Inca. Europeans encountered it during Columbus's voyages, and it spread worldwide, becoming a key crop for many cultures.

7. Curry:

Origin: The word "curry" is derived from the Tamil word "kari," meaning sauce or relish for rice. The concept of using a mix of spices to flavor dishes is ancient in South Asia, but the curry we recognize today has evolved over centuries with influences from Indian, British, and other cuisines.

8. Tomatoes:

Origin: Native to western South America and Central America, tomatoes were introduced to Europe by Spanish explorers in the 16th century. Initially, they were grown mainly for ornamental purposes due to fears they were poisonous. Their use in cooking took off in Italy, leading to dishes like pizza and pasta with tomato sauce.

9. Pasta:

Origin: While there's a myth that Marco Polo brought pasta back from China, pasta-like foods existed in Italy long before his time. The oldest Italian pasta factory dates back to the 4th century BC in Sicily, with the Etruscans having a form of pasta much earlier. However, pasta's widespread popularity and the pasta shapes we recognize today evolved over centuries in Italy.

10. Rice:

Origin: Rice has been cultivated in Asia for more than 10,000 years, with archaeological evidence from China suggesting rice domestication occurred around 8,000 years ago. Rice spread from Asia to the Middle East, Africa, and eventually to Europe and the Americas, becoming a staple food for billions.

11. Cheese:

Origin: Cheese-making likely began with the transportation of milk in animal stomachs, where rennet (an enzyme in the stomachs) would naturally curdle the milk. This tradition goes back to around 8,000 BC in Mesopotamia, with cheese becoming an integral part of diets in many cultures, each developing unique varieties.

12. Beer:

Origin: Beer brewing can be traced back to ancient civilizations. The Sumerians in Mesopotamia around 4,000 BC are known to have brewed beer, which they called "kash," and it played a significant role in their society. Evidence of brewing has also been found in ancient China, Egypt, and other regions, showing that beer was independently developed in different parts of the world.

13. Tacos:

Origin: The taco can be traced back to the 18th century in Mexico, where silver miners would wrap meat or fish in tortillas for a quick meal. The term "taco" referred to the small charges used to extract minerals, metaphorically similar to the small, rolled shape of the food.

14. Bread:

Origin: Bread-making began with the Neolithic Revolution when humans started farming and cultivating grains. The earliest bread was likely unleavened, flat, and made from barley, emmer, or einkorn wheat in ancient Egypt around 8,000 BC. Leavened bread, which uses yeast to rise, was developed later, with evidence from ancient Egypt suggesting that leavening began around 300 BC.

15. Bananas:

Origin: Bananas originated in Southeast Asia, possibly Papua New Guinea, where they were first domesticated around 8,000 to 5,000 BC. They spread through trade and migration across the Indian subcontinent, Africa, and eventually to the Americas during colonial times.

16. Chili Peppers:

Origin: Chili peppers are native to the Americas, with archaeological evidence of their cultivation dating back to 7,500 BC in the Tehuacán Valley of Mexico. They were spread around the world following Columbus's voyages, significantly impacting cuisines globally.

17. Apples:

Origin: Apples originated in Central Asia, in the region around modern-day Kazakhstan. Wild apples have been eaten for thousands of years, but domestication likely began around 3,000 BC. Apples were brought to other parts of the world by trade, particularly by the Romans, and later to the Americas by European colonists.

18. Kebabs:

Origin: The concept of skewering meat and grilling it can be traced back to the ancient Persians and Greeks. The word "kebab" comes from the Arabic "kabab," which might have originated from an earlier Aramaic word. This method of cooking was perfect for nomadic cultures, allowing for easy preparation and portability.

19. Hummus:

Origin: Hummus likely originated in the Middle East, with chickpeas being a staple in the region for thousands of years. The earliest known recipes for a chickpea spread similar to hummus can be traced back to 13th-century Egypt, but the dish has evolved and is now popular across the Middle East, with each country having its own variation.

20. Soy Sauce:

Origin: Soy sauce dates back to ancient China, with some historical accounts suggesting it was used as early as the Western Han Dynasty (206 BC – 220 AD). It was made by fermenting soybeans with wheat, salt, and water. Over time, its production spread to Japan, Korea, and Southeast Asia, each developing their own styles.

21. Tofu:

Origin: Tofu, or bean curd, was invented in China over 2,000 years ago during the Han Dynasty. It was created by Liu An, a prince of the Han Dynasty, as part of an effort to make food from soybeans during a time of famine.

22. Olives:

Origin: Olives have been cultivated in the Mediterranean region since the Bronze Age, with archaeological evidence from Crete dating back to 3,000 BC. They were not only a food source but also used for oil, which was vital for lighting, cooking, and religious rituals.

23. Ice Cream:

Origin: The origins of ice cream are debated, with various cultures claiming its invention. A form of ice cream was enjoyed in ancient China as early as 3000 BC, made from snow flavored with fruit, wine, or honey. However, the frozen dairy product we recognize today has roots in Italy during the Renaissance, with Catherine de' Medici introducing it to France in the 16th century.

24. Sausages:

Origin: Sausages were already popular in ancient times, with records from Sumerians, Babylonians, and Egyptians. The Romans were known for their love of sausages, and the word "sausage" comes from the Latin "salsus," meaning salted or preserved. Sausages were a way to utilize all parts of an animal, preserving meat before the advent of refrigeration.

25. Currywurst (Germany):

Origin: This popular German street food has a surprisingly recent origin. It was invented in Berlin in 1949 by Herta Heuwer, who mixed curry powder with tomato sauce to serve with sausages. This dish became emblematic of post-war German cuisine.

26. Tea:

Origin: Tea has been cultivated in China for thousands of years, with legends attributing its discovery to the Emperor Shennong around 2737 BC. From China, tea spread to other parts of Asia, and through trade routes like the Silk Road, it eventually reached Europe in the 17th century, becoming a global staple.

27. Quinoa:

Origin: Quinoa was domesticated in the Andes region of South America, in what is now Peru and Bolivia, over 3,000 years ago. It was a sacred food for the Inca civilization, known as "mother grain."

28. Waffles:

Origin: Waffles are thought to have originated in Ancient Greece, but the waffle we know today began in the Middle Ages with the introduction of the waffle iron in the late 14th century in Europe.

29. Sandwiches:

Origin: The sandwich is named after John Montagu, the 4th Earl of Sandwich, who, according to legend, ordered meat between two slices of bread so he could eat with one hand while continuing to play cards. However, the concept of placing food between bread slices dates back to Hillel the Elder in the 1st century BC, who is said to have made "Passover sandwiches" with bitter herbs and lamb.

30. Spaghetti:

Origin: While pasta itself is ancient, spaghetti is believed to have originated in Sicily in the 12th century, where it was introduced by Arab traders. The name "spaghetti" comes from the Italian word "spago," meaning "string" or "twine," describing its shape.

31. Noodles:

Origin: Noodles have a long history in Asia, with China being the likely origin. Archaeological evidence from Qinghai, China, dates back to 4,000 years ago, but the precise origin is debated. Noodles might have been made from millet or wheat in ancient times.

32. Maple Syrup:

Origin: Indigenous peoples in northeastern North America, particularly the Algonquian tribes, were the first to discover that maple sap could be boiled down to syrup. Europeans learned this process from the Native Americans, and commercial production began in the 19th century.

33. Cinnamon:

Origin: Cinnamon comes from the bark of the Cinnamomum tree, which is native to Sri Lanka (formerly Ceylon). It has been known in China since 2800 BC, used in embalming in ancient Egypt, and was highly prized in the spice trade between the 1st and 16th centuries.

34. Yogurt:

Origin: Yogurt's origins are thought to be in Central Asia or Mesopotamia around 5000 BC. It was likely discovered by accident when milk was stored in animal stomachs, which naturally fermented into yogurt due to the presence of bacteria.

35. Gelato:

Origin: Gelato, the Italian version of ice cream, has roots in Sicily where Arab traders brought their ice recipes during the Middle Ages. However, gelato as we know it today, with its denser texture due to lower butterfat and less air incorporation, developed in the Renaissance courts of Italy.

36. Burgers:

Origin: The concept of ground meat patties likely began in Europe, but the modern hamburger has its roots in the 19th-century United States. German immigrants brought their version of "Hamburg steak," which eventually evolved into what we recognize as the hamburger, particularly after being served at the 1904 St. Louis World's Fair.

37. Tamales:

Origin: Tamales come from Mesoamerica, where they were made by the Olmecs, Mayans, and later the Aztecs. They are made by steaming masa (a dough made from corn) wrapped in corn husks or banana leaves, often with fillings like meat or chilies, dating back over 10,000 years.

38. Naan:

Origin: Naan is an ancient Indian flatbread, with references found in ancient Indian texts from around 1200 AD. It's believed to have originated in Persia, spreading to India where it became a staple, especially in the north.

39. Cheesecake:

Origin: The earliest recorded cheesecake recipe can be traced back to ancient Greece, where it was served to athletes at the first Olympic games in 776 BC. The Romans adopted it and spread it throughout Europe as they expanded their empire.

40. Bagels:

Origin: Bagels are of Jewish origin, with their history linked to the Jewish communities in Poland. One story attributes their creation to commemorate the victory of King John III Sobieski over the Ottoman Empire in 1683, where the bagel's shape symbolizes the stirrup.

41. Croissants:

Origin: Despite being quintessentially French, the croissant actually has its roots in Austria. The kipferl, a crescent-shaped pastry, was brought to France by an Austrian officer, and over time, French bakers adapted it into the croissant we know today.

42. Barbecue:

Origin: Barbecue has deep roots in the Caribbean, where the Taino people used a method called "barbacoa" to slow-cook meat over an open fire on a wooden structure. This technique spread to other parts of the Americas and was adapted by various cultures, including African slaves in the Southern United States, leading to modern barbecue traditions.

43. Dumplings:

Origin: Dumplings are found in cuisines around the world, but one of the earliest forms comes from China where they've been eaten since around 200 BC during the Han Dynasty. The shape and fillings vary widely across cultures, from Italian ravioli to Polish pierogi.

44. Ketchup:

Origin: The original ketchup came from China, where it was a fish-based sauce called "ke-tsiap" or "kê-chiap." When it was brought to Europe and then to America, tomatoes were added to the recipe, evolving into the tomato-based condiment we know today.

45. Cheddar Cheese:

Origin: Cheddar cheese was first made in the village of Cheddar in Somerset, England, around the 12th century. It became widely popular due to its long shelf life and the way it could be stored in caves near Cheddar Gorge, which provided ideal aging conditions.

These foods reflect the rich tapestry of human history, where culinary traditions have evolved through cultural exchange, migration, trade, and innovation, contributing to the global food culture we enjoy today.

RARE AND UNUSUAL KNOWLEDGE

Strange Food Laws Around the World

Food laws can be a reflection of culture, tradition, health concerns, or historical quirks. Here are some of the more peculiar food laws from around the globe:

United States:

- **Gainesville, Georgia**: It's illegal to eat fried chicken with anything other than your fingers. This law was passed in 1961 to honor the town's status as the "Poultry Capital of the World," and while not strictly enforced, it's a fun nod to local pride.

- **California**: It's against the law to eat an orange in the bathtub. This law was supposedly put in place to prevent people from getting sick from the combination of citrus acid and bath salts, though its enforcement and origin are murky.

- **Oklahoma**: It's illegal to take a bite out of someone else's hamburger. This law seems aimed at personal space or property rights in an unusual context.

- **Louisiana**: Sending prank food deliveries is illegal. This law was enacted to prevent what's considered harassing or fraudulent deliveries, including pizzas and other foods.

Canada:

- **Montreal, Quebec**: You're forbidden from throwing snowballs at mailboxes, which could include those at the grocery stores or restaurants if interpreted broadly.

United Kingdom:

- **England**: Under the Salmon Act 1986, it's illegal to handle salmon in suspicious circumstances. This odd law was intended to prevent poaching but has led to humorous legal interpretations.

France:

- **School Ketchup Ban**: In an effort to preserve French culinary traditions, a law was introduced in 2011 that bans the serving of ketchup in school cafeterias, except for with fries, and even then, it's limited.

Italy:

- **Rome**: It's illegal to eat or drink near public buildings, churches, or monuments. This law aims to maintain the aesthetic appeal of historical sites.

- **Sardinia**: Casu Marzu, a cheese containing live maggots, was once banned due to health concerns. Although it's not strictly legal, enforcement varies, and it's still consumed.

Singapore:

- **Gum Ban**: Chewing gum was banned in Singapore in 1992, with exceptions only for therapeutic or dental reasons. The ban was enacted due to littering problems and maintenance issues with the MRT (Mass Rapid Transit) system.

Japan:

- **Slurping**: While not a law, slurping noodles loudly is considered polite because it shows appreciation for the meal. However, it's expected in formal dining contexts, showcasing a cultural expectation rather than a legal requirement.

Thailand:

- **Feeding Pigeons**: In Bangkok, it's illegal to feed pigeons in public spaces like parks or temples. This law was introduced to control the pigeon population and reduce the associated health and cleanliness issues.

Brazil:

- **Watermelon Ban**: In the town of Rio Claro, Brazil, it was once illegal to eat watermelon in public. This bizarre law was seemingly enacted to prevent the mess, with fines for those who violated it.

Sweden:

- **Candy Sales**: In Sweden, candy and sweets are not allowed to be sold to children under 18 unless they are purchased alongside other groceries, part of a broader initiative to combat childhood obesity.

Norway:

- **Cheese Powder**: Norway banned the use of Yellow #5 food coloring in macaroni and cheese, citing health concerns, even though other countries allow it with warnings.

Australia:

- **Moving Your Car While Eating**: In New South Wales, it's illegal to eat in your car if it means you're not in control of the vehicle, which could be interpreted as including eating while parked with the engine running.

India:

- **Eating Beef**: In several states of India, particularly those with strong Hindu populations, there are laws against the slaughter of cows and the sale or consumption of beef, reflecting religious sensitivities.

Russia:

- **Beer Classification**: Until recently, beer in Russia wasn't considered an alcoholic beverage if it had less than 10% alcohol content, which affected how it was regulated and sold.

Belgium:

- **Mussels**: There's a curious law in Brussels that mandates eating mussels with a fork and spoon, not with your hands, to maintain decorum.

Spain:

- **Bathing Suit Ban**: While not directly about food, this law affects tourists eating in beachside eateries. In some areas of Spain, like Majorca, it's illegal to wear bathing suits away from the beach, potentially affecting where you can eat.

Historical Diets That Might Shock You

Throughout history, human diets have varied greatly, shaped by availability, culture, health beliefs, and economic circumstances. Some historical diets might seem bizarre or even shocking by today's standards:

1. The Spartan Diet:

Sparta, Ancient Greece: Spartans were known for their austere lifestyle, which extended to their diet. Their food was simple, consisting mainly of barley, cheese, figs, and a black broth made from pork, blood, vinegar, and salt. This diet was designed to promote toughness and simplicity over luxury.

2. The Incan Diet:

Inca Empire, Present-day Peru: The Inca diet was revolutionary in terms of plant diversity. They consumed potatoes, quinoa, maize, and various Andean grains. What might shock us is the practice of chewing coca leaves for energy and to combat hunger and altitude sickness, a tradition still alive today but regulated in many parts of the world.

3. The Gladiator Diet:

Ancient Rome: Contrary to the popular belief that gladiators were fed meat to bulk up, archaeological evidence suggests their diet was mostly vegetarian. They consumed grains, legumes, and drank a barley drink called "posca." Their high ash content in bones indicates a diet rich in plant-based foods, chosen for endurance rather than bulk.

4. The Medieval European Diet:

Europe, Middle Ages: The diet of medieval peasants often included a lot of bread, ale, and vegetables, but what might be surprising is the consumption of ale from childhood. Beer was safer to drink than water due to boiling in the brewing process, which killed off pathogens.

5. The Roman Garum:

Ancient Rome: Romans had a taste for garum, a fermented fish sauce made from the entrails of mackerel or other small fish. This was a staple condiment, used in almost every dish, somewhat akin to how soy sauce is used in East Asian cuisine today.

6. The Tudor Diet:

England, 16th Century: The Tudors enjoyed a diet that would seem both lavish and horrifying. They ate swan, peacock, and even porpoise. Moreover, the practice of "spit-roasting" live animals like pigs was not uncommon at feasts, where the animal's squeals were part of the entertainment.

7. The Viking Diet:

Scandinavia, 8th-11th Century: Vikings consumed a diet heavy in meats (including horse, pig, and cattle), dairy, and fish, but they also ate a lot of fermented foods. Surströmming, a fermented Baltic herring with an extremely pungent smell, was part of their diet, which can be quite shocking to modern palates.

8. The Georgian Era's Sweet Tooth:

18th Century Britain: At a time when sugar was becoming more accessible, the Georgian diet was excessively sweet by today's standards. Meals were heavily sweetened, with sugar used in savory dishes, leading to health issues like tooth decay and diabetes that we now associate with modern diets.

9. The Polar Explorer's Diet:

Early 20th Century Expeditions: Explorers like Robert Falcon Scott and Roald Amundsen on their treks to the poles often resorted to diets of nearly pure animal fats and proteins, consuming seal, whale blubber, and pemmican (a mix of dried meat and fat). This diet was chosen for its high caloric content in the extreme cold but would be considered unhealthy and nutritionally unbalanced by today's standards.

10. The Ancient Egyptian Diet:

Egypt, 3100 BC – 30 BC: While the diet included grains, fruits, and vegetables, workers building the pyramids were given a daily ration of bread and beer, which was more substantial than it might sound. However, what might shock is that they occasionally ate ibis and other birds considered sacred or taboo in other cultures.

11. The Victorian Era's Food Adulteration:

Victorian England: The practice of adulterating food was rampant. Bread might be mixed with alum to make it whiter, milk watered down with chalk or plaster of Paris, and even tea was often mixed with used leaves, colored with lead chromate. This was before food purity laws, leading to numerous health hazards.

12. The Pre-Columbian Mesoamerican Diet:

Aztec, Maya Civilizations: They relied heavily on maize, beans, and squash but also consumed insects like grasshoppers and ants, and mushrooms, including hallucinogenic ones like psilocybin mushrooms, for religious ceremonies.

13. The Fasting and Feasting of Medieval Monks:

Medieval Europe: Monks followed strict fasting rules, often eating one meal a day, which might consist of bread, vegetables, and fish, but not meat, eggs, or dairy. However, their fasting periods could be broken by feasts that were as indulgent as they were austere, including rich foods and copious amounts of wine.

14. The Inuit Diet:

Arctic Regions: Traditionally, the Inuit diet was predominantly from animal sources, including raw or frozen fish and whale, seal, and caribou, often eaten raw to preserve nutrients. This diet, high in omega-3 fatty acids and vitamin D, was adapted to the extreme environment but would be very foreign to many today.

CHAPTER 10

LANGUAGE AND WORDS

Words with Surprising Origins

Language is a living entity, constantly evolving, and words often have origins that might surprise us. Here are some words with unexpected etymologies:

1. Nerd :

Origin: Initially, "nerd" was used in Dr. Seuss's book "If I Ran the Zoo" in 1950, describing a fictional, oddly looking creature. Its adoption into everyday language to mean someone overly studious or socially awkward came later. There's also a speculative connection to the name Mortimer Snerd, a character known for his foolishness, but Dr. Seuss's use seems to be the primary source.

2. Quiz :

Origin: One popular story, possibly apocryphal, claims that an Irish theater manager named Richard Daly bet he could introduce a nonsensical word into the English language, and "quiz" was the result. He supposedly paid people to write "quiz" on walls all over Dublin. However, the word's true origins are more likely from the Latin "qui es?" ("who are you?"), used in medieval English university slang.

3. Muscle :

Origin: The word "muscle" comes from the Latin "musculus," which means "little mouse." This bizarre etymology stems from the ancients' observation that some muscles, like the bicep, when flexed, resemble a small mouse moving under the skin.

4. Salary :

Origin: "Salary" derives from the Latin "salarium," which originally meant a soldier's payment for his salt. In ancient Rome, salt was a valuable commodity, and soldiers were sometimes paid in salt or given an allowance for it, hence the term.

5. Posh :

Origin: Commonly believed to come from "Port Out, Starboard Home," referring to the best cabins on ships going to and from India, which were cooler. However, this is a myth. The actual origin is uncertain, but it might be related to slang terms for "money" or "a dandy" in the late 19th century.

6. Grog :

Origin: Named after Admiral Edward Vernon, nicknamed "Old Grog" because of his grogram coat, who in 1740 ordered the Royal Navy's daily rum ration to be diluted with water to reduce drunkenness among sailors. The mixture became known as "grog."

7. Robot :

Origin: "Robot" comes from the Czech word "robota," meaning "forced labor" or "drudgery," and was first used in Karel Čapek's play "R.U.R." (Rossum's Universal Robots) in 1921. It was Čapek's brother Josef who suggested the word.

8. Clue :

Origin: From the Old English "clew" or "clue," which meant a ball of yarn or thread. It stems from the story of Theseus using a thread to find his way out of the Minotaur's labyrinth, hence "clue" came to mean something that guides or leads to a solution.

9. Nice :

Origin: The word "nice" has undergone significant semantic shifts. Originally from Latin "nescius" meaning "ignorant," it evolved through Old French as "nice," meaning "foolish" or "silly." Over centuries, it transformed to mean "precise" or "fastidious," and now it means "pleasant" or "kind."

10. Sandwich :

Origin: Named after John Montagu, the 4th Earl of Sandwich, who, in the 18th century, favored eating meat between slices of bread so he could continue playing cards or working without stopping for a meal. His habit caught on, and the "sandwich" was born.

11. Villain :

Origin: From the Latin "villanus," meaning "farmhand," related to "villa," or "farm." Over time, the term evolved from simply referring to someone of lower social status to someone who was morally reprehensible or an antagonist in stories.

12. Avocado :

Origin: The word comes from the Nahuatl word "āhuacatl," which also means "testicle," due to the fruit's shape. The name was adapted through Spanish as "aguacate," eventually becoming "avocado" in English.

13. Panic :

Origin: From the Greek god Pan, who was believed to cause sudden fear in people or animals, particularly when encountered alone in the wilderness. Thus, "panic" originally meant the terror inspired by Pan.

14. Gymnasium :

Origin: From the Greek "gymnasion," a place for exercise or physical training, from "gymnos," meaning "naked." In ancient Greece, athletes often trained and competed in the nude, hence the connection.

15. Lynch :

Origin: The origin of "lynch" is controversial, but it's often traced to Charles Lynch, a Virginia justice of the peace who, during the American Revolution, organized extrajudicial trials and punishments. The term doesn't necessarily imply hanging, originally referring to any kind of punishment without legal authority.

16. Boycott :

Origin: Named after Captain Charles Boycott, an English land agent in Ireland in the 19th century. When he refused to lower rents during the Land War, local people collectively refused to work for him or with him in any capacity, leading to the term "boycott."

17. Quarantine :

Origin: From the Italian "quaranta giorni," meaning "forty days." This was the length of time ships were required to isolate before passengers could disembark during the Black Death to prevent the spread of disease.

18. Gossip :

Origin: From the Old English "godsibb," which meant "godparent" or "sponsor in baptism." Over time, the term evolved as godparents were often involved in intimate family and community affairs, leading to the gossip we recognize today.

19. Shampoo :

Origin: From the Hindi word "chāmpo," which means "to knead" or "press," referring to the traditional head massage during hair washing. The British in India adopted and anglicized the term.

20. Whiskey :

Origin: Derived from the Gaelic "uisce beatha" or "uisge beatha," meaning "water of life." This phrase was later Anglicized to "whisky" or "whiskey," depending on the region.

21. Sarcasm :

Origin: From the Greek "sarkasmos," meaning "to tear flesh," metaphorically referring to the sharpness of sarcastic remarks that metaphorically cut or tear at someone.

22. Pajama :

Origin: From the Persian "pāy-jāma," which literally means "leg garment." It entered English via Hindi, where it also meant loose trousers tied at the waist.

23. Gherkin :

Origin: From the Dutch "gurken" or "kurkum," which might have originated from the old Slavic "gurka." The term was adapted into English through the trade of pickled cucumbers.

24. Tattoo :

Origin: From the Polynesian word "tatau," which means "to mark" or "to strike." The term was picked up by European explorers in the Pacific, like Captain Cook, and brought back to Western languages.

25. Berserk :

Origin: From the Old Norse "berserkr," meaning "bear-shirt," referring to warriors who fought with extreme fury, possibly in a trance-like state, thought to be inspired by or possessed by bears or wolves (referred to as "berserkergang").

26. Dollar :

Origin: From the German "Thaler," short for "Joachimsthaler," a coin minted from silver from the Joachimsthal (Joachim's Valley) mine in Bohemia. This evolved through Dutch "daler" into English "dollar."

27. Punch :

Origin: Not the action of hitting, but the drink. It comes from the Hindi "pānch," meaning "five," as the original punch contained five ingredients: alcohol (usually arrack), sugar, lemon, water, and tea or spices.

28. Ketchup :

Origin: Originally from the Chinese "kê-chiap" or "kôe-chiap," a fish sauce or pickled fish brine. When British traders encountered it, they adapted it into a sauce using tomatoes, which eventually became the ketchup we know today.

29. Hazard :

Origin: From the Arabic "al-zahr," meaning "the dice." It was introduced to the West through the Crusades and was originally a gambling game, which led to its use in English for any risky or uncertain situation.

30. Soccer :

Origin: An abbreviation of "association football," which was often called "socca" or "soccer" in late 19th-century England to distinguish it from rugby football. The term was popularized in the U.S. and elsewhere.

31. Sarcophagus :

Origin: From the Greek "sarx" meaning "flesh" and "phagien" meaning "to eat." Ancient Greeks believed that limestone sarcophagi could decompose the flesh of the dead, thus the name.

32. Quilt :

Origin: From the Latin "culcita," meaning "mattress" or "cushion." It evolved through Old French "cuilte" and Middle English "quilt," referring to the padded bedcover or garment.

33. Candy :

Origin: From the Arabic "qandī," which itself derives from the Persian "qand," meaning "sugar." It came into English via the Old French "candié," which referred to sugar crystallization.

34. Pyjama : (Alternate Spelling)

Origin: As mentioned, from Persian "pāy-jāma," but it's interesting to note the British spelling "pyjama" versus the American "pajama," showing how words can diverge in spelling across different English-speaking regions.

35. Peculiar :

Origin: From Latin "peculiaris," meaning "of one's own property," from "peculium," which was a child's private property in Roman law, especially money given by a father. Over time, it came to mean something unique or unusual, belonging specifically to someone.

36. Fiasco :

Origin: From the Italian "fiasco," which means "bottle" or "flask," used metaphorically to describe a complete failure in the theatrical sense, where an actor's performance might be so bad it's as if they are "carrying an empty bottle," i.e., having nothing to offer.

These examples highlight how language is not just a tool for communication but also a historical record of cultural exchanges, conquests, migrations, and the whims of linguistic evolution. The journey of words from their origins to their modern meanings often tells a story as fascinating as any folklore or legend.

Phrases That Have Changed Meanings Over Time

Language is dynamic, and phrases evolve as society changes. Here are some phrases whose meanings have shifted significantly over time:

1. Decimate :

Original Meaning: In Roman times, "decimate" meant to punish a group by executing one in ten members. It was a literal reduction by one-tenth, often used as a military discipline measure.

Current Use: Now, it's used more broadly to mean to destroy or severely damage a large portion, not necessarily one in ten.

2. Naughty :

Original Meaning: Derived from the Old English "nāwiht," meaning "nothing." It once meant "wicked" or "immoral," often used in a serious context.

Current Use: Today, "naughty" usually describes someone playfully or mildly bad, especially children, or behavior that's considered mildly improper but not seriously wrong.

3. Awful :

Original Meaning: From "awe," which implies something that inspires wonder or fear. "Awful" once meant "awe-inspiring" or "worthy of respect."

Current Use: It now means "very bad" or "unpleasant," a complete reversal from its original connotation.

4. Nice :

Original Meaning: As mentioned before, "nice" came from "nescius," meaning "ignorant" or "foolish" in Latin, then evolved to mean "fussy" or "precise" in Middle English.

Current Use: Now, "nice" means "pleasant," "agreeable," or "kind," a significant shift towards a positive attribute.

5. Egregious :

Original Meaning: From the Latin "egregius," meaning "outstanding" or "distinguished." It was used to denote something remarkable, usually in a positive sense.

Current Use: Today, "egregious" means conspicuously or outrageously bad or offensive, a complete flip in connotation.

6. Lynch :

Original Use: As noted, "lynch" initially referred to any form of punishment or execution without legal authority, not specifically hanging.

Current Use: Now predominantly used to describe the act of hanging someone without a legal trial, often with racial connotations due to historical context.

7. Gay :

Original Meaning: From Old English "gā," it meant "full of joy" or "carefree." It had positive connotations of happiness.

Current Use: While still retaining its original meaning in some contexts, "gay" primarily refers to homosexual, particularly male homosexual, or pertains to the LGBT+ community.

8. Intercourse :

Original Meaning: Derived from the Latin "intercursus," meaning "to run between," it referred to any form of communication or exchange between groups or individuals.

Current Use: Though still used in its original sense, it's now commonly associated with sexual intercourse, narrowing its meaning significantly.

9. Silly :

Original Meaning: From the Old English "sælig," meaning "happy," "blessed," or "pious." Over time, it shifted to denote naivety or foolishness.

Current Use: Today, "silly" means foolish, nonsensical, or lacking in seriousness, often used affectionately.

10. Awkward :

Original Meaning: From Old Norse "afúga," meaning "turned the wrong way," it initially referred to something crooked or off-kilter.

Current Use: Now it describes situations or behaviors that are uncomfortable, embarrassing, or clumsy.

11. Bulwark :

Original Meaning: From Middle Dutch "bolwerk," literally "bole work" (tree trunk fortification), it meant a defensive wall.

Current Use: While still used in the context of defense, it's now more metaphorically used to mean any strong protection or support.

12. Let :

Original Meaning: In Old English, "lettan" meant "to hinder" or "to obstruct." For example, "without let or hindrance" meant something could proceed unstopped.

Current Use: In modern usage, particularly in tennis, "let" means an interruption in play that does not count against the players, like a serve that hits the net but still lands in the service box.

13. Literally :

Original Meaning: Meant to describe something in a strictly literal manner, without exaggeration or metaphor.

Current Use: Often used hyperbolically to emphasize a point, where it actually means "figuratively" or "not literally," leading to debates over its correct usage.

14. Wicked :

Original Meaning: From Old English "wicca," it meant "evil" or "sorcerous."

Current Use: Especially in some regions like New England, it can mean "very" or "extremely" when used in phrases like "wicked cool."

15. Meat :

Original Meaning: In Old English, "mete" meant "food" in general, not specifically animal flesh.

Current Use: Now, "meat" almost exclusively refers to the flesh of animals used as food.

16. Brave :

Original Meaning: From the Italian "bravo," meaning "bold" or "fierce," often with a connotation of aggression or violence.

Current Use: Today, "brave" means courageously facing danger or fear, with a focus on moral courage rather than just physical boldness.

17. Misgiving :

Original Meaning: Literally meant "giving wrongly," implying doubt or suspicion rather than confidence.

Current Use: Still used to express doubt or apprehension about something, but the original sense of "wrongly giving" has faded.

These examples show how language reflects changes in society, culture, and values over time. The evolution of these phrases from their original meanings to their contemporary uses can often be traced back to shifts in societal norms, technological advancements, or simply the natural drift of language through use and misuse by speakers. Word meanings change as they are adapted to fit new contexts, sometimes leading to fascinating linguistic journeys.

The World's Most Difficult Languages to Learn

Determining which languages are the most difficult to learn for English speakers involves considering factors like script, grammar, phonetics, and cultural nuances. Here's a list of some languages often cited as particularly challenging:

1. Mandarin Chinese:

Script: Thousands of characters must be learned, each with multiple meanings depending on context.

Tones: Four main tones and a neutral tone can change word meanings entirely, making pronunciation critical.

Grammar: While the grammar is relatively simple, the use of measure words and the lack of verb conjugation can be tricky.

Cultural Elements: Deep cultural context in language use, including idioms and proverbs, adds to the complexity.

2. Arabic:

Script: Written from right to left, with many letters changing shape based on their position in a word.

Dialects: Significant variation between dialects, with Classical Arabic (used in literature and media) and numerous regional dialects for everyday conversation.

Grammar: Complex system of verb conjugations, dual forms, and a case system for nouns.

Phonetics: Includes sounds not found in English, like pharyngeal and emphatic consonants.

3. Japanese:

Scripts: Uses three writing systems: Hiragana, Katakana, and Kanji (adopted from Chinese characters), each with its own rules and contexts.

Honorifics: A complex system of politeness levels affects word choice and verb forms.

Pronunciation: Some sounds are difficult for English speakers, and pitch accent can alter meaning.

Grammar: Sentence structure is Subject-Object-Verb (SOV), unlike English's Subject-Verb-Object (SVO).

4. Korean:

Script: Hangul is phonetic and relatively easy to learn, but mastering it involves understanding syllable blocks and their arrangement.

Grammar: Agglutinative, with numerous verb and noun endings that change based on formality, tense, and mood.

Honorifics: Like Japanese, Korean has a sophisticated system of honorifics that must be learned for proper social interaction.

Phonetics: Some sounds are unique, like the double consonants and the distinction between aspirated and non-aspirated stops.

5. Icelandic:

Grammar: Four cases, three genders, and complex verb conjugations, including archaic forms not found in most modern European languages.

Vocabulary: Many words are long compounds, and the language retains many of its Old Norse characteristics.

Pronunciation: Includes sounds that are difficult for non-native speakers and can involve different pronunciations based on grammatical context.

6. Hungarian:

Grammar: One of the most complex with 18 grammatical cases, vowel harmony, and extensive use of suffixes.

Syntax: Word order can be quite flexible due to the case system, which can confuse learners used to fixed word order languages.

Phonetics: Contains sounds and consonant clusters that might be challenging for English speakers.

7. Finnish:

Grammar: 15 grammatical cases, agglutinative nature, and vowel harmony rules.

Words: Can be very long due to the agglutinative structure where suffixes are added to root words.

Pronunciation: Contains sounds like the "ng" at the beginning of words, which are unusual in English.

8. Navajo:

Verb Complexity: Verbs are highly complex, often incorporating subject, object, direct object, and other information into one word.

Tones and Stress: The language uses tone and stress differences that significantly affect meaning.

Syntax: Different from English, with a subject-verb-object order but often with variations.

9. Polish:

Grammar: Seven cases, three genders, and verb aspects can be daunting.

Pronunciation: Consonant clusters and sounds like the retroflex "r" can be challenging.

Spelling: While the alphabet is Latin-based, it includes diacritic marks, and spelling rules can be intricate.

10. Russian:

Cyrillic Alphabet: A different writing system from the Latin alphabet with its own set of characters and sounds.

Grammar: Six cases, three genders, and verb conjugation can be complex.

Pronunciation: Palatalization of consonants and sounds not present in English.

11. Thai:

Script: Unique alphabet with 44 consonants and 15 vowel symbols that can be written above, below, left, or right of consonants.

Tones: Five tones which change the meaning of words, making correct pronunciation essential.

Grammar: No conjugation for person or number, but particles and modifiers are used extensively.

12. Vietnamese:

Tones: Six tones can alter word meanings dramatically.

Grammar: Subject-Verb-Object order like English, but the use of classifiers and the lack of inflection can be challenging.

Script: Uses the Latin alphabet with diacritics for tones and vowels, but the way letters are pronounced can be very different from English.

13. Georgian:

Script: The Mkhedruli script, with 33 letters, can be visually and phonetically challenging.

Phonetics: Contains sounds not found in many languages, including ejective consonants.

Grammar: Ergative-absolutive alignment, which can be difficult for those used to nominative-accusative systems.

14. Basque:

Isolate Language: Not related to any other known language, making it linguistically unique.

Grammar: Agglutinative with a complex system of declensions and conjugations, including the use of ergative case.

Phonetics: Has some sounds not common in Indo-European languages.

15. Gaelic:

Pronunciation: Many sounds are not intuitive for English speakers, and word stress can vary.

Grammar: VSO (verb-subject-object) word order, numerous verbal tenses, and the use of lenition and eclipsis.

THANK YOU FOR READING

If you enjoyed this book and want more interesting knowledge, you can scan the QR code below:

SCAN QR CODE, OR VISIT:

www.mytruequiz.com/**factsbooks/**

Made in the USA
Columbia, SC
17 December 2024

49737639R00104